Get off Your High Horse and Walk.
Rediscovering Authenticity in a new way.

Slade Suiter

Graphic Illustrations by: Albert Lobo

Copyright © 2011 Slade Suiter
Slade Suiter Publishing
All rights reserved.

ISBN: 0615510264
ISBN-13: 9780615510262
Library of Congress Control Number: 2011933879
Slade Suiter Publishing, Omaha, NE

Warning!!!!

READING THE CONTENT OF THIS BOOK MAY PLACE YOUR LIES IN DANGER!

Dedication

To my wife, Assumpta, who saw me through the hard times, weathered me through stormy times, and loved me through the rest. To my wildly creative and off-center mother, Patricia, who taught me to be free while having my feet on the ground. To my dad, Jim, who taught me to "don't knock it until you try it" and to "look up into the trees." To my boy, Steven, who shows me that I am a good dad and the great freedom that comes within staying wonderfully and genuinely weird.

My legal name is Steven Suiter, however this is not my original name. When I was born, my parents named me Slade. They both liked it and it felt right to them; however, eventually they gave in to external disapproval and pressure from the hospital staff and extended family and changed it to a more acceptable, Steven. Since this is a book about authenticity I will now make an active choice and resort back to my authentic name. You can now call me Slade.

Table of Contents

Dedication	v
Foreword	ix
Acknowledgments	xi
Introduction	1
Chapter 1: The Stage Manager; Our Slippery Ego	7
Chapter 2: Our Modern Society: Our Modern Stage	11
Chapter 3: Rethinking Old Ways and Opening Yourself to Even Older Ways	17
Chapter 4: Getting Off My Horse	23
Chapter 5: The Liar's Tree Model	27
Chapter 6: Articulated Lies	31
Chapter 7: The Model	51
PART 1: The Liar's Side of the Model	55
PART 2: The Balanced Side of the Model	65
Chapter 8: On the Shoulders of Giants	75
Chapter 9: How Does This Model Show up in Our Lives?	79
Chapter 10: How Do We Get Unstuck from the Stickiness?	85
Conclusion	111
Request	115
Bibliography	117
Biography	119

Foreword

Slade Suiter's book addresses things that we just don't like to talk about. The greatest roadblock on the way to our authentic self, is our self-deception. Slade's dedication, passion, and unique approach in addressing this ego driven world comes alive in the pages you are about to read.

True happiness and harmony come from within. Our outer world is a reflection of our Inner world. If we want to find harmony, we must lower the mask of the ego and seek to know our true inner essence. It is important to give voice to our true self in order to understand and know our authentic desires, talents and life purpose. This takes courage and is not for the fainthearted.

Returning to your authenticity will unleash massive amounts of energy that was originally being spent on sustaining lies. With this new vigor, you have the opportunity to reinvest your energy toward creating the life that is really worth living.

Slade Suiter's work will help you rediscover more about yourself. Through this awareness you will begin an exciting journey toward rediscovering your authenticity.

Dr. Michelle Nielsen
Barcelona, Spain

Acknowledgments

Thank you, Dr. Michelle Nielsen, for your insightful forward, encouragement, and guidance.

Thank you, Albert Lobo (Graphic Illustrator). Your work captures and shines.

Thank you, Mercedes Fernandez, for chewing on this manuscript and pointing it and me in the right direction with love.

Thank you, Maryam Yassini, for your assistance with the title and the hot points of interest.

Thank you, Cesar Millan (dog whisperer). Your techniques also work on humans (being calm and assertive).

Thank you, Karen Van Grunsven, for your hospitality and honesty.

Thank you, Carein Everwijn (horse whisperer), who showed me authenticity and congruent style.

Thank you, Nao Konishi, for teaching me how to live on another planet, and for your tactful support.

Thank you, Neta Kafri, for opening your house and teaching me about the world of polarities.

Thank you, Father Rick Arkfeld, for walking with me and teaching me about life all the way up to your death. I'm still learning.

Introduction

One morning, a few years ago, I woke up with my heart pounding. It was about 3:00 a.m. I awoke from a dream so real that I could swear that I was there.

There was a large, gray, stone table. It looked as if the table was made from a huge old grinding mill stone and then turned on its side and elevated a bit. There were several people sitting around this table (I did not recognize them). There was neither talking nor silence at the table. It seemed as if people were talking in the background; however, most everyone was silent at the table. Somehow I knew (because it is my dream) that the people sitting around this table were of their pure essence, and if someone was speaking, everyone at the table was "open" to listen and to learn. This table somehow served as an intersection of the big truth that we all share. I remember that I had the gift to literally reach into each person and touch his or her essence. I also knew that it was my job to guide people to this table and have them take a seat.

Then I woke up.

Get off Your High Horse and Walk.

What is this book about?

1. Unconscious and unaware of your impact.

2. Conscious and still unaware of your impact.

3. Conscious and finally aware of your impact.

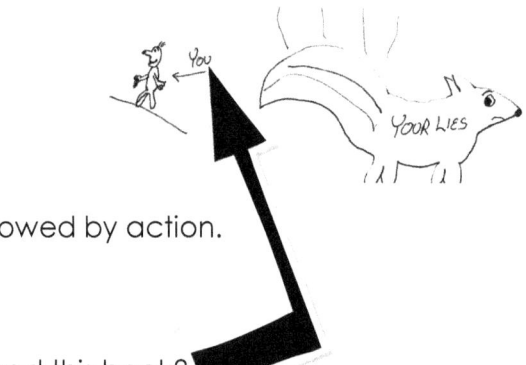

4. Choice followed by action.

Who should read this book?

Introduction

> *"A man is never more truthful than when he acknowledges himself a liar."*
>
> —Mark Twain

Liars and gentlecons and victims of all ages; we are all actors and liars. Whenever we hide our true selves from anything, it is a lie. This lie impacts everyone, not only ourselves. Whenever we hide behind our created self and projected images, which can include looks, power, religion, sex, or other masks, it is a lie. Most everyone knows this to be true and never dares to talk about it.

Have you ever caught yourself in a lie or bending the truth? Did you ask yourself, "Why did I just do that?" The reason will probably be difficult to nail down. Each lie is the result of something much deeper and bigger going on inside. This is where most people stop. They are afraid to look any further (not you, because you still have this book in your hands).

Self deception is like dirty underwear or a blister on our foot. You know it's ugly, and it is not going to go away by ignoring it or by pretending that it does not exist. Underwear needs to be cleaned, and the blister needs to be brought to the air where it can heal, so it is that we must be honest with our lies.

> *"Truth, like surgery, may hurt, but it cures."*
>
> —Han Suyin

There are many people who have invested large amounts of energy, time, money, and resources into projecting and building a false identity of who they are, only to find that they have become professional false actors. These individuals will find the message of true authenticity a threat to their own identity. They run the risk of discovering that perhaps an entire lifetime was dedicated to developing a false image of themselves. To these people, I offer an open hand with the invitation to be gentle with themselves and that, although difficult, it is a worthwhile and rewarding journey to rediscover your true self (your authenticity).

I am a qualified liar and actor. I am not a perfect liar (my wife can attest to that). I spent most of my life developing the art of unconscious deception and have been constantly performing, and, as I said, I believe most others are too. I have used this ability and unconsciously honed my skills to fit into a crazy world that demanded my performance. As a result, I gradually began to recognize that I was on stage and trying to perform for something false. In turn, the more I tried to "act," the more unhappy I became. It was as if I was selling out everything for my performance so that I could be an acceptable person.

> *"The privilege of a lifetime is to become who you truly are."*
> —Carl Gustav Jung

When self-deception is blocking me from my authenticity, and if I want to be authentic, I must do the following:

- **Recognize** (take my blindfold off) that I have been lying to myself.
- **Accept** responsibility (remove the clothespin from my nose) and experience first-hand the impact my self-deception has on myself and others.
- **Choose** to do something about it.
- **Do** something about it.

This book is about moving from recognition to action. Don't worry; I will hold your hand through this process—not as a guide, but like another blind person holding your hand on our way to the ophthalmologist.

A word of caution: reading past this point will most probably destroy the complacency of your life as you know it. Whether for better or for worse, that is for you to

Introduction

decide. Like the characters in the movie *The Matrix*, you have a decision to make. You can be content living your current life of lies, or you can decide to see yourself as you really are.

I am making several assumptions. You are human, so I assume that you are somewhat balanced and have an inkling of intellect. I am also assuming that you are on stage most of the time and that you are a liar.

> *So don't worry about tomorrow, for tomorrow will bring its own worries. Today's trouble is enough for today.*
>
> —Jesus Christ

CHAPTER 1:

The Stage Manager: Our Slippery Ego

"All the world's a stage, and all men and women merely players; They have their exits and their entrances, One man in his time plays many parts."

—Shakespeare

Many of us have a definition of the ego that may match that described by Carl Jung or Sigmund Freud.

Sigmund Freud created a model based on three interacting parts: the id, the ego, and the superego. The id is related to your instinctual drives, basic urges and passions. The ego is related to your reason and consciousness, while the superego (the moral police) is watching your ego's every move, ready to bash it over the head with guilt and shame.

Carl Jung presented an ego model that has four primary functions or ways of perceiving: intuition, sensation, feeling, and thinking. The external expression is defined by introversion and extroversion. Carl Jung's work is the basis of the Meyers-Briggs® personality profile.

> *Poverty comes from the people buying into the collective lie that, "we are powerless." It only takes one, to show this lie is false*
>
> —Ambassador Dennis Awori, *Chairman of Toyota East Africa*

My intention is not to refute the great works and thought that have gone before. I ask you to set aside what you already know about the ego, at least while you are reading this book. Open yourself up to a different understanding in order to gain a new perspective of how we work inside.

> *When you cover a seed with soil, it struggles to find the sun.*
> —Jim Suiter

The idea here is not to demonize or make your ego into a monster. Rather, your ego exists to protect you from a hostile environment and fulfill your basic needs for external validation and acceptance.

Until recently, this world has done little to develop and support consciousness, which means that society (our normal everyday environment) has been favorable in forcing people to resort to lies and self-deception. Our consciousness correlates to the degree to which we are aware of and connected to our essence, "our authenticity." We can think of consciousness as being in "hibernation." It's as if we were on an airplane and the pilots became sleepy and decided to take a nap, and before taking their nap, they engage the autopilot. Our ego is similar to the autopilot.

A hostile environment that is inhospitable to consciousness also promotes the ego by rewarding individuals who engage in self-deception. Our consciousness continues to sleep, and the ego has a fertile ground to take root and grow.

If the pilot is asleep, who is flying the plane? The autopilot function does not have the plane's destination in mind. It is simply programmed to keep the plane safe and react only to potential threats and obstacles. There is no true intelligence guiding the plane while the autopilot is engaged. Your ego steps in to this "autopilot" role.

Your ego prides itself in its stealth and the ability to stay hidden, and it desires to remain in the background unnoticed. Unfortunately, we need to shine a spotlight and see the ego for what it really is.

Your ego is well practiced at playing the following roles:

- **Personal Judge**
  * Your Personal Judge is responsible for casting judgment, labeling, blaming, and finding fault in yourself and others.
- **Stage Manager**
  * Your Personal Stage Manager ensures that you take the stage and dutifully wear your false mask.

Your ego is a part of yourself and reinforced by society. It is afraid, because it is aware that if you ever become conscious (meaning aware and awake), it will lose its purpose for existing. Your ego has a lot to lose if you truly become authentic. Your ego is facing annihilation, and who would not fight tooth and nail to survive?

> *"I think when one has been angry for a very long time then it becomes like old leather, and finally so familiar that one can't remember feeling any other way."*
>
> —John Luke Picard
> *(Captain Starship USS Enterprise)*

This book is not asking you to fight. We will take an approach that will hamper your ego's capacity to fight against you as it has in the past.

Chapter Summary
- See your ego in a new light and perspective. Your ego is active and exists because you were asleep. It has assumed control, because your true self did not. Your ego is trying to protect you, while at the same time it provides you with a steady diet of fear, thereby ensuring its survival.
- Your ego's main roles are Personal Judge and Personal Stage Manager.

CHAPTER 2:

Our Modern Society: Our Modern Stage

Imagine that I went to my kitchen and started to melt down bag after bag of sugar. I added brown food coloring, cooled it, flattened it, and ingrained lines. Now I have something that very much resembles wood.

Is it wood? No, it's not. It is an imitation, something false. It is a lie.

Can you construct something on top of it? Of course you can, as many of us do.

What happens to what you build on top of this false foundation, this "sugar wood"? Nothing, until it rains.

The foundation is the most important part of any construction. If the foundation is false, building anything on top of it is folly. No matter what you build, and no matter the quality and the strength of the materials that you use, you will constantly need to fix this and that so that things don't fall apart. It requires great attention and focus. In the end, it will fall. Your ego has a lumberyard of "sugar wood" (so sweet!), and it is just for you.

> *Experience: that most brutal of teachers. But you learn, my God do you learn*
> —C. S. Lewis

Whatever is built on a false platform, no matter how appealing in appearance, it is fundamentally a lie.

Remember the ego roles of Personal Judge and Personal Stage Manager? The primary job of your ego is to convince you that you are not OK as you are. When you buy into this deception, you have only one choice: you need to find validation from the outside.

Much of our energy is spent trying to con others into believing that we are something different from who we really are. We do this in order to fit in, to be accepted, or to be successful to our public audience.

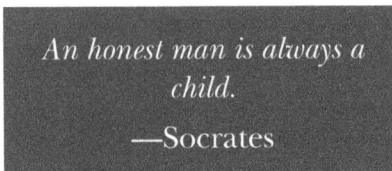

An honest man is always a child.

—Socrates

Please allow me to reintroduce to you an old and well-known acquaintance of ours, Ms. Society. She is a bit concerned with shining any light on the ego, and she wanted to offer her viewpoint.

So without any further delay I hand you over to Ms. Society.

Thank you, Slade. Now, listen up closely readers. That includes you! I am here to teach you how to be successfully accepted by your society. You can always find a part to play. The requirements are few and simple.

I strongly discourage anyone from even thinking of using your intuition. That "silly voice" will only lead you into needless turmoil and strife. Constantly swimming against the current and moving against the grain will exhaust your poor little self. We can't have that now, can we?

Any rebellious activity, such as challenging one of society's victims, confronting society's bullies, "telling your truth," or any activity that may be interpreted as disturbing "liar's bliss" will be dealt with swiftly and harshly. You will be labeled as "one of those individuals." You will be judged and found guilty of disturbing our societal norms. We will have to punish you.

Stating your truths and being honest will be viewed as heresy. I will personally see to it that society rejects you. You will not be able to fit in. You will become the strange one. There were many people before you who did not fit in; Mahatma Gandhi, Abraham Lincoln, Martin Luther King Junior, Nelson Mandela, and Rosa Parks. Do you want to join the likes of them?

Enough of that, you get the point. As long as you subscribe to one of the "lies" that Slade listed here in this book, you will fit in just fine.

Just look at all that society has to offer for those who follow the rules. You can look forward to the constant and vital competition and limited resources that will invigorate you and give you purpose. We have the finest instructors available to you at the Blame Institute. You will never have to be accountable for your actions again! Enrollment is free. You can inform yourself with news that caters to morbid curiosity and that offers you a smorgasbord of all-you-can-eat murders and scandals. If disaster presents itself, or if there is something that you should fear, I assure you that you will not miss it. The fashion industry will do all it can to convince you that you are ugly. Politicians tell you "the way it will be," you know it won't and you will elect them anyway. Soap operas expand the web of lies and corrosive gossip—you can safely sit back and compare your life to the drama. Commercials eloquently help your children decide what they need (and they didn't even know that they needed it!). With all that society offers you, why would you choose anything else?

End of lesson.

> *To shed the mask, and let yourself be naked.*
>
> —Amir-Esmaeil Bozorgzadeh

Thank you, Ms. Society. I am sure our readers will keep your words in mind. Society will always do its part to prepare a role for us to play.

We live a duality, an incongruent life behind masks and images that we create, while trying to not lose ourselves. We create a habit of playing to our audience while not meaning what we say and not saying what we mean. We constantly project an image for others, and this image changes depending upon our situation, who we are talking to, and what we hope to gain out of the situation. Each time we project an image that is not ourselves, it is false, a lie.

Chances are that this includes you, and chances are that you know this to be true. This knowledge comes from a place of authenticity that tells you that this is true. When you hear a truth, you know it. This "place of authenticity" is your ultimate objective.

I am calling you a liar without accusation; I am merely speaking a truth that you already know. There is no blame.

You're not alone. Everyone struggles with honesty, and the people who are consciously aware of their self-deception are far and few in between.

Fear is the big paralyzer. We are fearful of our own truths. What if you took an inventory of the beliefs that you truly believe in? What if these personal truths set you apart from your family, your loved ones, your religion, and your childhood beliefs? Just imagine the ammunition the enemies (whom you created) would have if they knew your personal truths!

> *A man should look for what is, and not for what he thinks should be.*
> —Albert Einstein

We say and do all sorts of things to protect, isolate, and insulate our true selves from others. We travel far and take extraordinary actions that are not true in order for people to see us as OK, to gain their approval or pats on the head. How did we learn to lie with such fluidity? What is it like to live in a cycle of lies? More importantly, how do we break this cycle? What does it feel like to access our essence, our authenticity? How can we be authentic while not judging others or ourselves?

Collective movements toward authenticity

In the past, people who became their true selves were seen as unpredictable and hard to control. Many innocent people were imprisoned or even burned at the stake for voicing their truths and beliefs in centuries past. They threatened rigid governments and belief systems.

Even though awareness means swimming upstream in today's complex society, the world as a whole is becoming more receptive to authenticity.

The hippies of the 1960s and 1970s were big on the ideas of consciousness and "it's cool to be yourself." I always thought that my eldest sisters were hippies, and I don't think that they were aware of it. I am a "hippie wannabe"—I love the tie-dyed clothes, long hair, peace signs, braided beads, and bare feet.

> *Authenticity is actually something that unfolds in the moment. It begins by having some sophistication with the vast territory of the self and then, in the moment, having the courage and commitment to be real.*
>
> —Karen Kimsey-House

The hippies accepted and embraced people regardless of color, faith, or sex. They wanted an end to segregation, which contributed to the 1963 March on Washington. They promoted peace and love.

From the 1980s to the present, consciousness movements have given rise to peer mentoring, life coaching, slow food, simplifying life, and so on.

Today, the concept of consciousness has received a push from the global economic crisis. Many people for the first time are being forced to adapt their lifestyles and are opening to the possibilities of new and smarter ways of living. The culture is much more receptive to awareness and consciousness. Where are you at now?

I invite you to do what is necessary to find your sense of humor: being able to laugh at yourself will enable you to overcome the protection mechanisms your ego designed to protect itself. I am not referring to destructive humor, where many people hide behind sarcastic veiled attacks. I am referring to a healthy and constructively curious self-humor, that we can use with ourselves, others, and situations. Think about the last time that you felt rigid, stuck, and closed to other ideas. Where was your healthy sense of humor then? It is very difficult to stay rigid while having

> *Any fool can criticize, condemn and complain and most fools do.*
> —Benjamin Franklin

a sense of humor. The reason for this is that your humor dissipates rigidity and provides a lighter perspective in which you can see yourself in a new way that just was not available before. So, activate it. It is easy for people to label and categorize others who are different from themselves. If you decide to pursue your authenticity, it is possible that you may be labeled "strange" and different." I happily invite you to accept the title as you earn it.

People are easy to trick. We often believe the lies we hear, not because they are convincing, but because the ego needs lies to exist.

Chapter Summary
- If you build anything on a false foundation, in the end, it will itself be false and will fall down.
- We spend so much energy trying to fit in because we are listening to an ego that tells us, "You are not OK as you are." Ms. Society paints a picture of superficiality by saying, "Conformity has benefits."
- You are a liar, and you are not alone. Society is a duality of incongruence. You are soft and vulnerable inside. We all are, but we work hard to convince others that we are not. It is time to be honest. Swallow the pill of honesty and admit that you are not that honest.
- You are lucky to be living today. History was not so kind for those seeking authenticity. You will most likely not be burned at the stake for voicing independent ideas, but you may be labeled as "different, or maybe even strange."
- One of the greatest qualities of being a human is having a sense of humor. Rigidity will get you nowhere. Find your sense of humor and activate it. It's a wonderful path around the ego's defenses.

CHAPTER 3:

Rethinking Old Ways And Opening Yourself To Even Older Ways

Let us open the window and flush the toilet on *political correctness*. Let's remove some of the barriers that prevent us from seeing truth.

Political correctness is a mass and subjective belief that any possible offensive language and practices regarding gender and race should be eliminated.

> *The truth may make you free, but there's an even chance it will first scare the daylights out of you.*
>
> —Gregg LeVoy

Like martial law, political correctness confines creative resourcefulness and is designed to control social behavior. It is like setting rules down for children who cannot be trusted: "Because we can't trust you, we must apply the following rules and regulations."

There may have been a place and time for martial law as well as political correctness, but if we are to move forward as a human race, we need to set an intention to continue to move forward in our expectations of humanity.

It is difficult to be honest when we set up safeguards to protect ourselves from hearing a truth. I ask you to distance yourself from political correctness so that you can gain a new perspective.

Replace *political correctness* with *common respect* and hold common respect as a higher human virtue.

Common respect encompasses all that political correctness is trying to achieve and yet has no need for categorizing or labeling. There is no need to hide behind socially imposed walls designed to separate special or victimized individuals from others. There is no need to categorize and label. Respect is big enough to encompass all concepts, people, and situations, and it begins with you.

I can decide not to do something simply because I was told not to and that I would be punished for doing it. This shows an external locus of control. On the other hand, I can decide not to do something because I have common respect for myself and others, and this comes from my place of authenticity. This shows an internal locus of control.

> *The test of authenticity is whether you can remain mindful of the desire to appease people who may not like what the authentic version of your self has to say.*
> —Nick Kettles

What does it mean to be present? To be present means to not live in the future or the past. It means to live in the present moment, right where you are at this moment and to allow yourself to be there fully. Most spiritual texts and religions have "presence" as one of the most important focal points for life itself. There are many writings and various exercises on how to achieve living in the present moment.

I want to offer a different perspective on how we can arrive to living in the present. First of all to be living in the present should not be seen as an end or as an objective. I would like you to consider that "being present" is a mere by-product. Being present is a by-product of your authenticity, meaning when you are truly authentic you are present and consciously aware of not only yourself, but of everything around you.

So the focus is not how to be present, rather how to be authentic. The approach to authenticity is rather simple.

To remove any and all obstacles that stand in your way, between where you are now and your authentic self. The obstacles that stand in your way are primarily the lies that you say to yourself, your self-deception.

Let me give you a feeling of what I am talking about, It is a crisp and crystalline day, you are standing on a hill, and off in the distance is a mountain that captures your attention. This mountain is breathtaking and its beauty moves you so deeply you can't seem to move your eyes from it. You feel very present and notice the vibrant contrasting colors against the dark blue sky and the building cumulus clouds to your left. Your connection to this mountain is of deep feelings and not words. The next day you search for this mountain and all you see is the gray misty fog that has set in during the night. You remember the feelings of the beauty, however, there is nothing to be seen.

> *Go, fly, free yourself!*
> *Live your life with joy!*
> *No time to waste, yet enough time to get your job done!*
>
> —Nao Konishi
> 小西 奈緒 15

Did the mountain disappear? No, it is still there. Why can you not see it? The misty fog has blocked your vision and has left you with limited perception. What do you need to do to see that beautiful mountain again? Wait until this fog lifts.

The fog is your obstacle to the mountain, as your lies are your obstacle to your authentic self. The difference is you needed to wait passively until the fog lifts in order to see the mountain, whereas you can actively participate in dismantling your lies in order to arrive to your authentic self.

Freedom in difference

Is standing out such a bad thing?

I believe there is something valuable we can learn from the following fictional characters.

- SpongeBob Square Pants and Patrick the Starfish from the cartoon, *SpongeBob Square Pants*
- Sid the Sloth from the movie *Ice Age*
- Forrest Gump from the movie *Forrest Gump*
- *Tater the toe-truck from the movie Cars 1 & 2*

What do these characters have in common? They do not take things personally. They are highly successful in what they set out to do, they all seem to be living in the present moment, and they are a bit different, strange.

> *Man will occasionally stumble over the truth, but usually manages to pick himself up, walk over or around it, and carry on.*
> —Winston Churchill

They don't "fit in" because they live outside society's conventions and expectations. If you have watched the films or animations, you will see that there are plenty of people around who cast judgment on them. See for yourself, which people come to mind in your own life that have these qualities. How do you feel in their presence?

Part of their freedom is their acceptance of their individual strangeness for the sake of remaining true to themselves. So what if you don't fit in? Who is happy and free?

As you rediscover your authenticity, and allow it to take shape. It is likely that some individuals may not accept you as they once did. You will most likely receive some new titles and labels. If the cost of becoming yourself earns you the label of "strange" or "different," embrace it. Wear it as a validation of your progress to authenticity.

I have always felt comfortable in the presence of people who "beat their drum to a different rhythm." I find the feeling of being able to "let down my hair" and share my true feelings liberating. In the presence of such individuals, there is no expectation to act a certain way.

Having the courage to speak your truth may also earn you respect and admiration from the people around you. They, like you, will recognize authenticity when they see it.

Chapter Summary
- Replace political correctness with common respect. Give the morality police a vacation. Let us treat humanity as though it is "coming of age." We are ready to adopt common respect as the new way of dealing with each other.
- Living in the "present moment" (presence) means not living in the future or past, and being fully here in this moment. Don't allow "presence" to be your end objective; rather, see presence as a natural by-product (something that happens naturally) when you truly become your authentic self. Let your pursuit of authenticity be your focus. Work on eliminating the lies that stand between you and becoming your authentic self.

  > *If I speak up I am condemned; if I stay silent I am damned.*
  > —Jean Valjean
  > *(Les Miserables)*

- Authenticity comes with a price, but don't fear it. You will most likely be labeled strange, different, or weird and stand out in a different way for seeking authenticity as your way of life. These titles give you enormous latitude of behavior and freedoms that other people who "sell out" do not enjoy.

CHAPTER 4:

Getting Off My Horse

One of the most important lessons I learned about authenticity came from horses. You can´t lie to horses. They see right through you.

I went to Tokyo to offer a leadership workshop with a dear friend of mine, Nao Konishi. This was a two-day workshop designed to bridge the cultural gap between parents and their children living in Tokyo, and we had all sorts of crazy things planned. Everything turned upside down, and nothing came out the way it was expected to. Between a flu outbreak and a typhoon, many participants were cancelling. We decided to go ahead with the workshop with whoever showed up.

> *Authenticity: be yourself, be transparent, if you don´t know who you are then be courageous enough to find out, it is your right to truly realize your magnificence!*
>
> —Priya Hallam

One of the planned activities involved working with horses. The leaders of the workshop and the owners of the stables were dripping with rain and ankle-deep in mud as they showed the participants how to develop confidence with a horse. We received positive feedback despite the bad weather. The horses played a big part in it, and we considered the workshop a success.

I was curious about the horses and wanted to know more. My friend Karen introduced me to a "horse whisperer" named Carien Everwijn from the Netherlands. I made an appointment to visit her and her well-known healing horses. Her horses are like natural emotional barometers that help people to regain confidence in themselves and others.

When I arrived, Carien explained how these horses help people. She explained that everything about a horse and its genetic makeup prompts it to run away. They are "flight" animals, thus making them sensitive to everything around them, including emotion and intention.

She mentioned that humans often prejudge and are incongruent (we lie to ourselves), which becomes a problem when our internal feelings do not match our external behavior.

> *Am I not destroying my enemies when I make friends of them?*
> —Abraham Lincoln

Horses accept authentic and congruent emotions. After she explained this, I was apprehensive about meeting the horses—part of me did not want them to see that I was "putting on a show." Carien immediately saw that I did not know how to let go of my image and that I was afraid that her horses would confirm this.

It became clear that the reason I was there was to confront my double message, my incongruence. The animals innately detect the energy and intentions behind our words and actions.

She introduced me to the horses and asked me to do several exercises in which they rejected me and did not allow me to join the herd (ouch!). Let me explain why this hurt. One of the horses' main objectives is to ensure the safety of the herd. This includes rejecting any horses that they view as unstable or unbalanced (incongruent). So, here I was rejected by the herd, with a hurt prideful ego.

I can understand that this may sound strange to people who have never worked with horses.

I felt frustrated and busted! They were not buying it. I was trying my best to project an image of leadership and certainty. Perhaps I was saying to myself, "If I can snow these horses, I can fool anyone," but the horses would not give me an inch. They wouldn't budge. They stood there and looked at me as if they were saying, "Do you think that we are stupid or something?"

Carien asked, "Slade, what happened?" I told her how I felt inside, and how I felt like a failure, and that I was frightened to connect with the horses. It was difficult for me to know when I was being authentic. She suggested that I stop "trying" and, as a first step, simply to connect with the horse. "What does that mean?" I asked. She said, "To see the horse as it is, to drop your agenda about what you are trying to do."

> *I would say authenticity could be experienced as: Fearlessly being the most unadulterated version of YOU with no effort to control how that may land on the other side of your personal universe!*
>
> —Angie Hoole

She told me that these horses are trying to do everything in their power to reach out and connect with us, and most of the time, we are the ones blocking them. She said, "All nature is trying to do the same. We humans are not allowing this connection." She went on to say that my intuition was correct. The horse was challenging me, but not in the way that I was interpreting it. She suggested that I approach the horse with a sense of wanting to play with the challenge—something like two brothers who are sharing the backseat of a car on a long trip—and see what happens.

Knowing that the horses were doing everything that they could to reach out to me made a big difference. All I needed to do was allow that to happen. I was the one who was prejudging and mistrusting them. I told the horse that I was clueless about what I was doing, that I

> *Who am I? What do I know?*
> *I Love you. That's it.*
> —Ann Betz

felt a little screwed up on the inside, and that I was going to be here until I succeeded in connecting with him. We performed many exercises. Eventually the horses let me into the herd (meaning that they found me to be congruent) and eventually even offered me a chance to lead the herd (meaning to take the position of the lead horse) when I least expected it.

At the end of my experience, Carien asked, "What made it work for you?" I said, "The fact that they are reaching out to me and that I did not have to try." I told her that the only way I could describe it was "coming home."

This book is the result of that coming home experience. Plato referred to this experience as *remigro*, which means to wander back, to come back, to return. You return to a place that you already know.

Chapter Summary
- Humans often prejudge and show incongruity (lying to ourselves). Horses and other animals reject incongruent behavior. To communicate with them, drop the pretense; we must allow what we feel on the inside to show on the outside.
- Horses and all living creatures are doing everything in their power to communicate with us. All you need to do is allow this communication to happen. Drop your agenda and see things and situations as they really are.
- *Remigro* is a Latin word that means to wander back, to come back, to return.

CHAPTER 5:

The Liar's Tree Model

The Liar's Tree model has come to my mind from the alchemy of two ideas sprinkled with my experience and forged into a new direction. The first idea is derived from the fields of psychology and psychoanalysis: the inferiority complex and the superiority complex, where a person, usually on the unconscious level, feels either inferior or superior to another affecting his or her behavior and subsequent interaction with others. The second idea is from a book called: *The Anatomy of Peace: Resolving the Heart of Conflict*. The book refers to different boxes that we unconsciously place ourselves into. They include a "less than" box, a "more than" box, and a "need to be seen as" box. Thus, I present to you the Liar's Tree.

> *Who is more foolish, the child afraid of the dark or the man afraid of the light?*
>
> —Maurice Freehill

Notice that this tree has one trunk, which is divided into three main branches, which in turn are divided into the foliage. The roots remain hidden inside. They feed all the lies and represent the fear, "I am nothing." Above the roots is the trunk of the tree, which contains the biggest lie. It is responsible for all the lies that come after it. The biggest lie is "I am not OK as I am," including all my perceived flaws, faults, failures, and brokenness.

After accepting this lie (I am not OK as I am), we progress up the tree to one of the three main branches. You can choose from Superiority, Inferiority, and Please Validate Me. From there, you proceed to the foliage, which includes the articulated lies that you use (the ego trap) to protect yourself and so that others do not discover that you are not OK as you are.

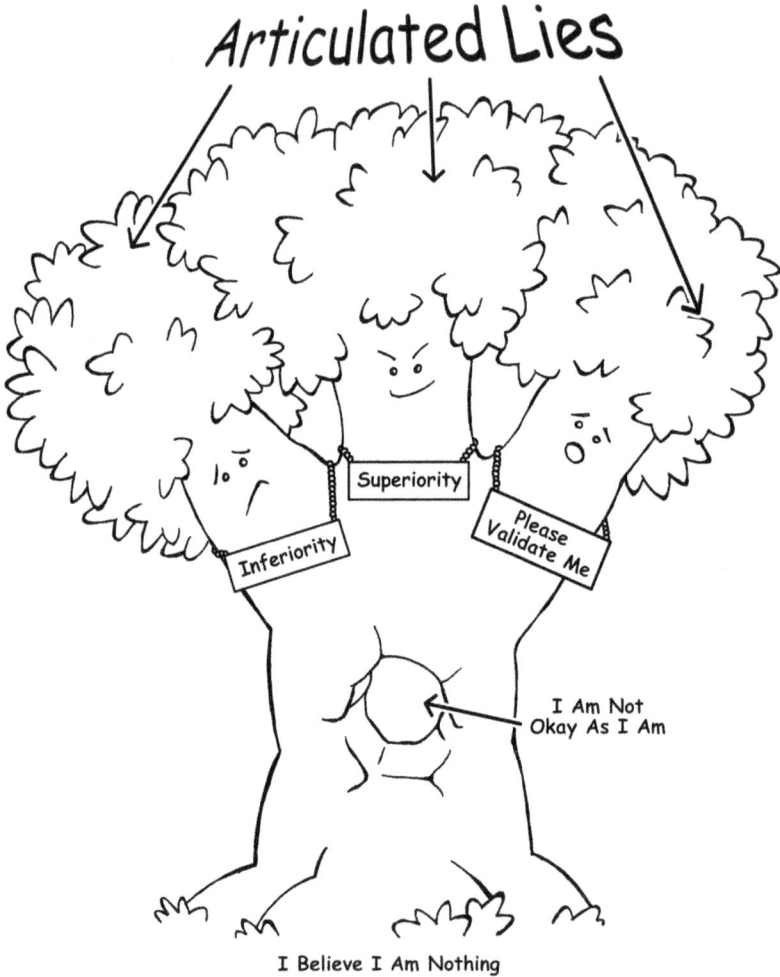

Many of us believe the root lie "I am nothing," because it is based on a partial truth. Your ego's worst fear is the realization that it does not exist. Your ego will aggressively protect itself to ensure its own existence.

Chapter Summary

The Liar's Tree works like this:
- The root lie is "I am nothing." I have no value, I am not important, I am insignificant.
- The trunk lie is "I am not OK as I am," including all my faults, weaknesses, and failures.
- The branch one lie is Superiority.
- The branch two lie is Inferiority.
- The branch three lie is Please Validate Me.
- The leaves and foliage are the individual lies (articulated lies).
- Your ego is active in the lower parts of the tree. It wants to convince you that you are nothing and that you are not OK as you are, that you need to project something that you're not.

> *We should start by observing how animals act. They are honest and appreciate it when we are honest with them. If you present something nice to an animal in one hand while hiding a rope in the other, the creature will know your intention. Yet animals have no religion, no constitution. Basic nature has endowed them with the faculty of discernment. It is the same for humans.*
>
> —Dalai Lama

CHAPTER 6:

Articulated Lies

The articulated lies illustrate unconscious behaviors and attitudes that frequently show up in everyday life. This section shines a spotlight on our consciousness to discover the skeletons hanging out in our closets.

> *Never never ever say never.*
> —PMS (Patricia Marie Suiter)

Recall the three branches of The Liar's Tree:
1. Please validate me. (These people are like sponges to be filled.)
2. I'm superior. (These people are like stealthy wolves on the prowl.)
3. I'm inferior. (These people are like vampires, vultures, or leeches who refill their energy by taking from others.)

Category of Lies: "Please Validate Me"

The following lies are under the category, "please validate me" because these individuals will try many tactics in order to gain external validation of who they are as individuals.

Barbie and Ken

Image is everything for these people. Narcissist city. Their lies are based on society's ideals of beauty and success. Barbie and Ken feel the need to project a perfect image of themselves to fulfill this prescription. These individuals choose a superficial and shallow view of the world. They have an air of phoniness, and they are careful to create situations where they will be safe and comfortable. Seeking out individuals who will support their perfect image is important to them.

How do these people feel about living this lie?

Everything I say and do must convince you that I am who I want you to see. I must admit that I am spending most of my energy in doing so. Just go to my Web page, or Facebook profile, or blog, and you will read about how good I am and about my altruistic ideas for saving the world. How could you not praise me for that? I have dedicated a lot of time in surrounding myself with people who accept my way of being—"Look perfect in every area." I am uncomfortable with discussions of religion and politics and philosophies that differ from my own, and do my best to avoid people that differ from my views. I see what society wants of me, and I'm going to become it. My greatest fear is that you will see the "disordered-mess" I feel inside. I do not feel confident as I am, so I project the perfect image that "they" want to see. If people see me as perfect, there's nothing to criticize or judge. If others do not criticize me, then I must be OK, and thus I am validated.

> *Happiness is not something ready made. It comes from your own actions.*
> —Dalai Lama

VIP Membership

There is nothing wrong with wanting to belong to a group, but the reason for wanting to belong can be a lie.

People who buy into this lie join any groups associated with social prestige and power such as country clubs, yacht clubs, and other "power associations." They choose these groups not because they want to or because they believe in them but because of something that they lack. The motivations are "Please validate me" and "I must join because all the important people belong."

Have you ever seen people who join protests and strikes without knowing what they're protesting against? It is attractive to get lost in the collective power of a crowd and to claim this power as their own.

How do these people feel about living this lie?

I belong to the "foo foo" club. They all love me, like you should. At the very least you should admire me. Heaven knows I need it. I have such low self-confidence that I need to bask in the warm glow of associating myself with important people. I feel insecure and vulnerable. I have not spent much time developing my own ideas or beliefs, my own sense of identity. I am somebody when I'm with people who are somebody. I enjoy laughing when they laugh. I feel as if I am climbing in life because of the "somebodies" I keep company with. Surely this makes me somebody too. Doesn't it?

> *To believe in something, and not to live it, is dishonest.*
> —Mohandas Gandhi

Yes Fish

A Yes Fish seeks external validation by placating. Just as a chameleon changes its colors to fit its environment, these people have highly developed skills of adaptation to suit the expectations of the audience in front of them. They have repressed their personal convictions for the sake of approval. Yes Fish people are seen as hypocritical and difficult to trust. They may say yes to your face, but when you turn your back, you might hear the truth. Dictators love Yes Fish, because they do not have to instill fear to gain their loyalty. The Yes Fish are seeking external approval to validate that they are OK.

Yes Fish in the workplace feed the management what they want to hear and do so while withholding the truth. If you want to see if this lie is active in your business, look for stagnation, your employees "just doing a day's work," lack of creativity, and a cloud of fear that prevents anyone from challenging the status quo.

How do these people feel about living this lie?

I feel hollow and that my words are not worth much. I am great in social occasions; I bounce from person to person, telling each one what he wants to hear. I choose the path of least resistance and bend my words to please you. I am like a soothing balm for people who want to be lied to. I am sure you can recognize me at your place of work, in your family, or giving political speeches. Even though I flip-flop with my convictions, many people choose to listen to me. I honestly do not value my own word. If I ever stood up to voice what I truly believed, I fear I would be rejected or crushed underfoot.

> *Get your facts first, then you can distort them as you please.*
> —Mark Twain

Sun Drops (White Lies)

You would not believe the number of people who defend "sun drop lies." They say, "These are lies designed to save another person's feelings; is that not a worthy objective? It is worth the cost of a little lie. Who does it hurt anyway?"

I still use these lies but less often than I did before. However, this question may bother you enough to pause before you tell a sun drop lie. What is the intention for it? What is your reason behind it? Do you have confidence in the person that you are lying to? Perhaps the use of sun drops is a reflection that you do not have confidence in yourself. Will the person benefit by hearing it? What is your motivation for not offering your truth?

Let's say that I just purchased a pair of pants and asked you for your opinion. They look horrible, with funky patterns and clashing colors that make me look fat. "They are nice," you say. How will this lie serve me when I go to the party I bought them for? What if I wanted to know your honest opinion? Sun drop lies are examples of "Please validate me" needs, because they keep you in a good light.

I sometimes tell sun drop lies, but the people I am honest with seem to return to me with more respect than if I offered them a lie. However it is important to have the correct intention to truly help and serve that person while being as empathetic as I can.

> *Being your real self with all the colors, shadows, clouds and diversities we have inside us and reflecting them to the outside. It is our wholly beings.*
>
> —Souzan Bachir

How do these people feel about living this lie?

I do not have the confidence to tell the person in front of me the truth he or she just asked of me. I (your author) fail a lot here; however, the people I am honest with seem to return to me in time with more respect than if I offered them a lie that they wanted to hear...I'm trying to do better. And I do know that sun drops is a gateway to becoming a yes fish. Just think of that. (Hmmmmmmm)

Prostitutes Are Us

We sell ourselves in so many ways. We tend to get so caught up with the literal definition of prostitution that we forget the core of what prostitution is. Whenever I compromise my personal ethics, values, or personal truth to achieve money, power, or notoriety, I am a prostitute. Prostitution in your personal life or the workplace is risky business. Individuals sell personal values and stretch ethics for the sake of the bottom line (business image and profit). In many instances, businessmen and businesswomen present an image that is not their true self. This makes it convenient for them to go to work and prostitute their values, saying, "All in the name of business."

How do these people feel about living this lie?

What I do is no one else's business. If I sell out and no one else knows it, I am not hurting anyone. If I want something material or recognition and acceptance, I know how to get it. All I have to do is to sell. My supervisor and co-workers decide to withhold information from the consumer on one of the products that we sell. I want their approval, and raise my hand when they ask who will support the idea. I feel uneasy making such a decision, but my ego justifies the action by telling me, "Everyone does it." Even though I justify my actions, I have difficulty looking people in the eye, and I have a hard time falling asleep.

> The truth is the kindest thing we can give folks in the end.
> —Harriet Beecher Stowe

Drama Queen/King

Drama Queens spend their lives waiting for the other shoe to drop. They expect drama. The law of attraction (like energy will attract like energy) will not disappoint them and will provide a constant stream of frantic life issues.

These individuals want to be sucked up in the tornadoes of drama and doing things to feel alive. They enjoy exaggerating stories that reflect the importance on the storyteller. Meaning is tied up in emergencies, live soap operas, and any event that takes the stage. It doesn't matter whether they play the hero or the victim; what matters is that the chaos of their lives is sure to impress themselves and others.

How do these people feel about living this lie?

Do not let the storm finish and the dust settle. Keep stirring the waters. I do not wish to be seen by others or myself. I look forward to somebody asking how I am. I choose not to see life as it is; I prefer to see the fantasy. Anything that sounds important and big, I am there. Victim or hero? I can play both, or I may just play the storyteller. It doesn't matter as long as there is drama involved. The sense of vibrating urgency will distract me from my inadequacies. If I can feel the blood coursing through my veins, the adrenaline in my system, my heart pounding for the new love in my arms, or my heart torn to shreds in a devastating tragedy, I feel validated and alive. Balance is of little interest to me. I much prefer to live in the extreme polarities of life, because that is where the action is. It is where I find purpose. Just ask me how I am, and you will find out.

> *A lie cannot live.*
> —Martin Luther King, Jr.

Rolling Stone

These individuals find meaning in being busy. Movement serves as a distraction from looking at themselves. Daily routines and new activities are attractive to the Rolling Stones, because they offer security and an exterior sense of purpose.

How do these people feel about living this lie?

I am not gathering moss; I have purpose. Can't you see how busy I am? Look at me move. Those shirts must be ironed right after phoning the dentist, and then off I go to work, dropping off my kids on the way. I don't have time to look inside myself, and if I do have a moment free, I pick up the telephone and call someone, anyone. My life is built on the slow quicksand of sadness, melancholy, and/or guilt. I need to keep moving, because the alternative is that I begin to sink until I become paralyzed. Be careful around me, because I will judge you according to my standards of busyness. You must be as purposeful as I am. Idle hands are the devil's workshop.

Cry Me a River (The Professional Victim)

Victims go through a natural process of grief, and suffering is normal and healthy. The Cry me a River victim is a person who chooses to remain in a place of disempowerment instead of moving on.

> *Authenticity is what the world needs now...*
>
> *It is for me to daily clarify to who I am, and to why I am here, and to proceed accordingly with positive energy.*
>
> —Paulette Genthon
> (Director UCHA)

Cry Me a River people are professional victims. They enjoy talking about their misfortunes, pains, sufferings, and misery. This is an attractive lie, because it absolves them from personal responsibility. As an added bonus, it gives them a sense of meaning and purpose through their misfortune. Professional victims are running rampant in today's society and take shelter in the shadow of political correctness. You can recognize them because they have leech-like qualities. They need to find individuals to attach themselves to, because they need a steady supply of pity and attention. They find a willing participant or a person who is not able to say no. They attach themselves to that person's compassion, and they suck out time, energy, and compassion as long as the host will allow them.

How do these people feel about living this lie?

Poor me! The reason for my actions is because "this" happened to me and "that" happened to me. I always have an excuse for being the way I am. I choose to hide in this place of disempowerment and pity because I have a reason to be here, and no one is going to take that from me. As long as you continue to agree that I have a right to hide, I will suck your energy and enjoy the benefits of your pity and attention. It is important that you see that I am a "less than" person. I say, "poor me," you say "poor you," and we are in business.

Ditto Bug

What kinds of lies were you told as a child? In Miguel Ruiz's book, *The Four Agreements*, domestication is an unwanted process of unconscious agreements. This is a transparent lie (difficult to see), and because it is so invisible, it touches most of us. We do not choose where we are born. We did not have much say-so during birth, did we? We received many things by chance, depending on when and where we were born. We did not choose our birth parents, the country we were born into, the religion we were taught, nor our primary education. We were told how to live a good life and how to be a good girl or good boy. We accepted what others said. I like to call this the lie of immaturity.

> *Common sense is the knack of seeing things as they are, and doing things as they ought to be done.*
>
> —Stowe

Chances are that there was a multitude of lies hidden in your upbringing. The lies were mixed in with many truths. We sift out the lies from the truth, in every area of life. Many religions choose to label and separate others. Entire countries may hide injustice and tyranny within their laws. Our educational systems may have taught us biased lessons. Our parents may have taught us lies by their actions or projected their own agendas on us. We must filter out what we choose to believe from what was given to us from childhood. When you choose to consciously agree with something that you have learned, it becomes a true (authentic) belief.

How do these people feel about living this lie?

What do you want me to do? I have believed this way my entire life. My mother and father, my teachers at school, my religion, and country told me how to live and what to believe. How could I question the things that I have believed in so deeply and for so long? I am a product, and I will remain a product of what I was told to be. If I questioned these ideas, I might discover that what I held on to so tightly all these years was a lie. Then what?

Category of Lies: Inferiority
Kick Me

Kick Me is a composite lie that has two manifestations. There is either a complete unconscious element or an awareness of being an "active" deception. Individuals who experience this lie feel deep guilt, blame, unworthiness, and an unconscious need to punish themselves. Invalidation can be a thought or a feeling or both. This lie can be active as a thought and as passive as an unconscious feeling. It can come from years of conditioning and believing "I am not OK as I am" and remain hidden in the subconscious. A Kick Me personality can also arise from a single traumatic episode or violation.

> *Speak with your own words, live in your own way.*
> —Marta Giménez

How do these people feel about living this lie?

I feel like The Cowardly Lion in the Wizard of Oz. By nature, the lion is suppose to be strong, proud, and courageous, but I feel weak, ashamed, and afraid. I have a sense of hopelessness, a sense of "if I could just make it through another day." I often feel like I want to be invisible. This prevents me from stepping up and taking responsibility for who I am. I am content to live in obscurity and in the shadows of those around me. I will accept misfortune and abuse from others because I feel unworthy and ashamed about who I am. It seems to feel right somehow that I am punished. You will not be able to find me living this lie, because I am determined to maintain my distance and invisibility.

Under the Sleeve

These individuals can be known as "distraction artists." They have learned the art of shifting attention or focus away from them. They are happy to be involved in a conversation as long as it has little to do with them. When the conversation shifts to their direction, they eloquently deflect it in another direction. (Note that the ability to deflect is not always a lie. In fact, the skill is useful in dealing with negative people and situations such as offering a distraction for people with Alzheimer's.) "Under the Sleeve" becomes a lie when the intention of the individual is to hide the true self. Almost like a magician, someone not paying attention may not notice anything. That's the way the Under the Sleeve people want it. They masterfully bend and shift situations not of their liking to the direction of their choosing. They are difficult to catch unless you stay attentive to the conversation at hand. To see examples of deflection, watch a political news conference closely, and see if the politicians indeed answer the question they are asked.

> *Employ your time in improving yourself by other men's writings, so that you shall gain easily what others have labored hard for.*
>
> —Socrates

How do these people feel about living this lie?

The image I project is important to me. I need complete control most of the time. I fear the power people would gain over me if they saw me for who I really am. I do not feel like putting my true ideas out there or having to answer for my actions. If I'm in an argument in which I fear that I am losing ground, I pull out a mirror and hold it up before the person or somewhere else. I run away to cover up my deficiencies, and I don't want anyone but me to know it.

Head in the Sand

This person is similar to Yes Fish in that both of them hide from confrontation; the difference is that Yes Fish agrees with whoever happens to be there at the time. Individuals with their head in the sand choose not to see the lies that they are living. If they don't hear or see it, it must not be real. This is a lie of denial that usually has to do with wanting to remain stuck, powerless, and stagnant.

How do these people feel about living this lie?

I am not going to be the one creating problems. I can let it go, and it won't bother me if I didn't see it. It's much easier to pacify aggressive behavior, to accept personal attacks, and to tolerate disrespect from others. I continue to absorb it like a sponge. I want to keep the peace. After all, I spent a lifetime doing it. What good would it do if I spoke my mind now? They would just turn their attacks on me, as they always do. I know there is injustice, and I just look away. I feel helpless, disempowered, sad, and physically ill; my stomach ties into knots. My face and posture reflect how I feel inside. You will recognize me not by my actions but by my inactions and the perverse pride I have in my ability to accept and tolerate abuse. You may also catch me playing "head in the sand" as an "altruistic" way of sacrificing myself for others.

> *Authenticity is: Congruence. Literally "being" inside out.*
> —Biba Binotti

Category of Lies: "Superiority"
Slave Master

On the surface, these people appear to be self-confident and in control. Creating a front for others is important to them. The Slave Masters' purpose is to dominate, to turn people into objects, and eventually control and own them. Their lie is poisonous and destructive. They will work hard to gain footholds (leverage) in your life that they can turn and use against you. Their main objective is to dehumanize you to a degree that they can justify using you. These individuals have low self-confidence and are cowards, thus creating the need to control those who are close to them. Because they do not trust themselves, they cannot trust those around them. These individuals work hard at distancing themselves emotionally to see people as objects (usually the people who would be closest to them). The Slave Masters embody the ego's tools for control. They feel satisfaction when people succumb

> *The chief cause of human error is to be found in prejudices picked up in childhood*
> —Descartes

to their power. They attack, sabotage, blackmail, and manipulate people and situations to ensure control. They often act out of shame and guilt and feel justified in treating others in the same way that they treat themselves.

How do these people feel about living this lie?

I feel the fires of jealousy burning in my stomach. I am insecure, but you will not know this, because I invest most of my energy controlling and sabotaging your individuality and freedom for the security that comes with "my" control. If you are not one of my victims, you may see me as a charming person. I give myself permission to treat you any way that I see fit based on my sense of insecurity, because I do not see you as an individual person with rights. I can turn you into an object to be used and controlled in a drop of a hat. I must admit that I'm confused about the boundaries between love, sex, and power. If I feel that I own you, I will punish anyone who tries to challenge my control. Try it and you will see.

Echo Echo

These individuals have a strong need to compare and compete. This can be a subtle lie that can hide in "motivating" someone to achieve, to succeed, or to outdo others in life and work. This person will compare income, houses, careers, spouses, number of children, education, and so on.

How do these people feel about living this lie?

My main focus is myself, using you as my mirror. My fear is being left behind. My life is not my own, as you are indirectly directing my life. If you have two children, I'm going to have three. What grade did you get on the final? My dad's stronger than your dad. I have to buy that dress that just came out, because you do not have it yet. I need to keep up with you and outdo you. I enjoy it when you fail, because if you are happy or successful, it is easier for me to tear you down so that you can feel the misery that I live in.

Blind Mice

These individuals are afraid of everything that is different from them. They are instructed by their society, culture, religion, or schools to fear anyone whose skin, culture, or creed is different. They are prone to be prejudiced, to be ethnocentric, and to buy into fundamentalism.

> *The mind is everything. What you think you become.*
> —Buddha

They are easy to recognize by their intolerance of anyone challenging their beliefs. They are willing to forfeit individual thought and reason to adhere to external ideas. These are people who are lost inside themselves and react to potential threats out of fear of guilt or punishment.

How do these people feel about living this lie?

I was brought up to believe in a certain way, so don't come to me with new ideas or ask me to think for myself. I do not have the right to think for myself. If I do, I will be punished, condemned, or damned, and I'm afraid. I view everyone who does not share my beliefs as a threat and a potential enemy. Watch out! "Whoever is not with me is against me."

The Cat's Claw

Individuals who lie with the Cat's Claw attempt to gain power and worthiness through the demise of other people. These are premeditated lies and indirect attacks that allow the aggressors to hide their intentions. If they are confronted, they may say, "Oh, I'm sorry, that was unintentional," or "You are taking things too personally, you are too sensitive."

Think of a cat catching you by surprise and viciously scratching you. You are bleeding and hurt. When you turn to confront the cat, you see that the cat has already retracted its claws. The cat looks at you as if to say, "What in the world are you talking about?" This type of person may attack you directly or is just as likely to indirectly engage in gossip about you behind your back. The book *Pride and Prejudice* includes great examples of the Cat's Claw in action.

> *Authenticity is a state of freedom and peace that touches our hearts and minds that is reflected in our words and actions.*
>
> —Paridokht, Ishani

How do these people feel about living this lie?

I don't feel good about myself. I am terrified that people will be able to see my weakness. Do not be fooled by my pleasant smile and tone of voice, as they are honey to lure you in for the kill. I love the smell of blood. The more I hurt you, the better I feel. Don't worry, you won't be able to touch me, as I have seen to that. I have already covered my attack with words that can't be traced back to me. I can't stand it when you feel better than I do, so I will see to it that you feel like I feel when I'm done with you.

The Small God

These individuals are the center of the universe. They are almighty and powerful, and they busy themselves in creating their domain as they see fit. People become objects to be used for their convenience. Because they answer to no one outside of themselves, they are free to judge, find guilty, and punish anyone who displeases them. They believe in no one but themselves. They are highly egotistical and do not care who knows it.

How do these people feel about living this lie?

Get off Your High Horse and Walk.

You scratch my back, and you can just keep on scratching. I deserve it! I live my life like an immortal. I can do what I want, when I want, and where I want to do it. No one has the right to tell me no. If you try to tell me that I was spoiled as a child and got everything that I wanted, I will not listen to you. Everything would be great if I just didn't feel so alone. I feel like there is a big hole in me that can't be filled. I feel like no one understands me, and I'm afraid that no one ever will, but I sure in hell will not let you know that. So, I am content when people properly respond to my power. I have spent years believing myself to be a god, so you had better do the same. If you don't, I will become angry and threatened, and it is my duty to punish you. I deserve more than normal mortals.

> *If we are made in the image and likeness of God, then it follows that God has one great sense of humor.*
> —Slade Suiter

Now that you have read through the lies did certain people come to mind as you read these descriptions? Did you find an individual that fits each category? Note that it is possible to have a combination of lies going on at the same time, for example being a ditto bug and a prostitute, or a small god with the cat's claw. Reread them, and then consider if or how the categories of lies may be active in your life.

I can write about these lies, because I have recognize many of them in myself and others around me. I still struggle. I realized that each lie takes me further away from my essence (my authentic self). The idea is not to live a life devoid of excitement but to become aware of the lies. Please keep balance in mind, each lie separates us further from our essence (our authenticity).

Write them down and ask yourself, what impact have I been making on others? DO THIS WITHOUT ONE DROP OF JUDGMENT or labeling. Know that this is a gift that you're giving yourself to grow. This will give you an opportunity to see yourself in the cycle of lies that may have been holding you back.

> *False words are not only evil in themselves, but they infect the soul with evil.*
> —Socrates

Bittersweet Time Line

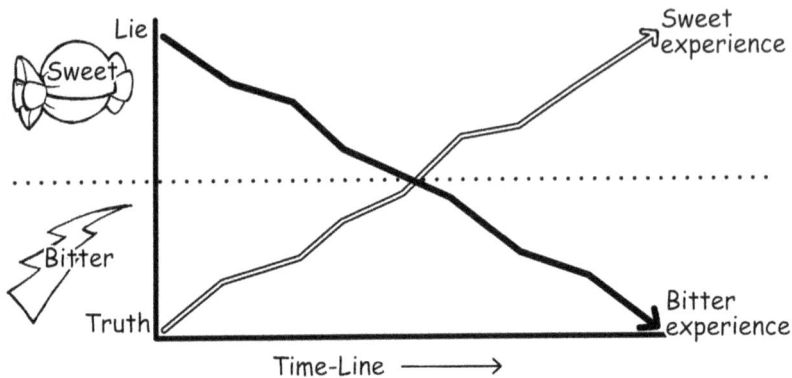

Check the bittersweet time line against your own experience. You may find it uncomfortable when you speak or act according to your truth to the point that the experience is bitter. This is especially true when you put yourself "out there" or confront someone.

I had to confront someone over a lack of respect. I tried my best to prepare for it, and I rehearsed, listening to my tone of voice. I felt every fiber in my body tighten. The confrontation went as I had expected: terrible. It was messy with hurt feelings, bruised egos, and plenty of counterattacks. I tried hard to stay with my truth that I felt without judgment, but I still felt terrible after the confrontation and physically and emotionally drained. It was a bitter experience. As time passed, I noticed that the person shifted, and I noticed more respect in many areas. She now shows respect in ways that definitely were not there before, and I have a newfound respect for her and myself. Eventually, the experience turned better and sweeter.

I could have done what I had done in the past. I could have continued to say, "It doesn't bother me so much." My lie would have let me off the hook of confronting her. That would have been easier. However, the lack of respect would be sure to happen again, and I would feel disdain for my inability to confront her. Even if a lie started out sweetly, getting me off the hook, in time, it would turn bitter.

What did you experience when you chose to voice a difficult truth? Was it sweet or bitter for you? Did you notice a bitters-or-sweet change over time?

> *A question that sometimes drives me hazy: am I or are the others crazy?*
>
> —Albert Einstein

Chapter Summary
- Articulated lies are divided into three categories: Superiority, Inferiority, and Please Validate Me.
- Time is your friend; saying your truth often begins bitter, and a lie often begins sweet. Use your experience to see where it will end. In time, the truth will eventually turn sweet, whereas the lie will become bitter.

Please Validate Me: Barbie and Ken, VIP Membership, Yes Fish, Sun Drops, Prostitutes Are Us, Drama Queen/King, Rolling Stone, Cry Me A River, Ditto Bug

Superiority: Slave Master, Echo Echo, Blind Mice, The Cat's Claw, The Small God

Inferiority: Kick Me, Under the Sleeve, Head in the Sand

CHAPTER 7:

The Model

"When you are content to be simply yourself and don't compare or compete, everybody will respect you."

—Lao Tzu

I experienced "coming home" when I got off Carein's horse and started walking on my own feet. I felt a deep desire to explain with words what I was feeling. This was tricky, because there are no words in this place. It is experiential, the feeling of coming home, the experience of expansion, the place where truth lives. In short, it is that "you are" and "I am" exist only in the now.

All one "place"

The great philosophers employed reason and logic to arrive at this place. Spiritual leaders and theologians use parables to sneak past the defenses of the mind, so that the stories invoke personal experiences that are tied to a truth. Poets use allegories and poems that give rise to an experience that is tied to that place. Painters express the experience of that place on canvas. Composers create from this place, for it is in this place that senses take on meaning. They hear where there are no words. They see without using their eyes. They feel, they create, and we experience that place. Genius creates and understands from this place. Children launch their imagination from this place.

> *Lying makes a problem part of the future; truth makes a problem part of the past.*
>
> —Rick Pitino

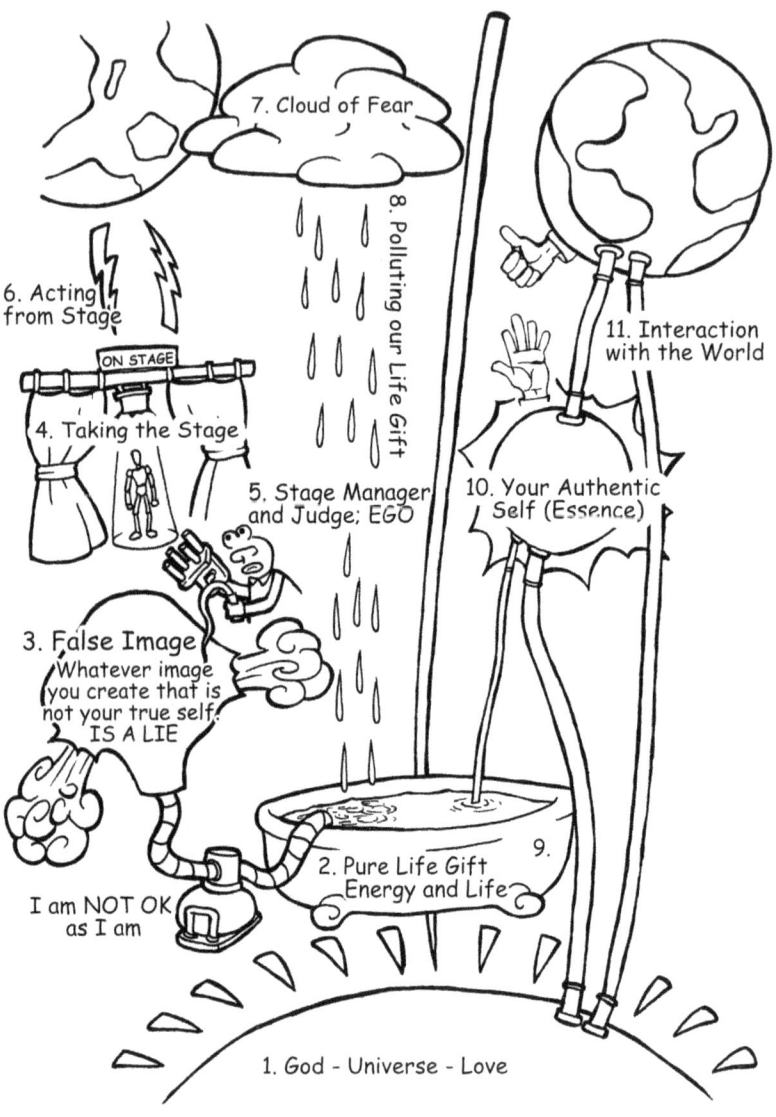

This place is our destination, for it is where we will find true authenticity.

The components of the following model already existed; it was built on the shoulders of great philosophers, artists, writers, and theologians and strange people like us. The model is a visual demonstration of what happens when we lie and when we are honest, what it means to be authentic, and especially what it means to be inauthentic.

I first presented this model to my twelve-year-old son. I was on the floor with papers and arrows, and he walked in. He said, "Daddy, you are so weird." I said, "Yes, I am. Look at this model. Does it make sense to you?" He looked at it for a moment, shook his head, and said, "Yes, I understand it, and you're still weird." I had the beginnings of a working model that a child could understand. I had to dip way deep into my experience to draw this model, and I have tied together many great lessons from my favorite authors and spiritual texts. It is here to give a new perspective of what happens when we get tangled up in our lies.

> *Authenticity, when your soul sees the light, and your body walks towards it.*
> —Martin Richards

MODEL PARTS

1. God-Universe

This is where you recognize and acknowledge something bigger than you. For many people, this will be Being, God, Love, Higher Power, Universe, One Power, Energy, Mother Earth, Father Sky, etc.

2. Pure life gift—this is where the model begins in relation to you

Take two fingers and place them on your carotid artery located on your neck; the pulse that you feel means that you are alive. There's nothing you did to receive or earn life. It is a gift.

Your pure-life-gift energy is like a swimming pool, or bathtub that is refilled every day. This basic holding tank or bathtub is not unique only to humankind. Everything that is alive also shares in this bathtub of cyclical energy. This "bathtub" does not take into account a conscious connection between the individual and other people, nor does it take in to account a conscious connection between the individual and God-Universe. Thus absolutely everyone and everybody regardless of their personal understandings and beliefs all share in this one same pure-life-gift. (This is an important piece to remember because this bathtub will come into play as a "limited resource of energy" by individuals living on the "liar's side of the model." This will also will be an important connection point to reach out and connect to individuals who are unconsciously deceiving themselves.)

> *A house divided against itself cannot stand.*
> —Abraham Lincoln

You have a basic certain and quantifiable amount of energy available to you each day. For example, if you wake up in the morning and decide to run up Mount Everest, the moment that you collapse from exhaustion is when you have depleted your life-gift-energy (you get the idea). This tub is not limited to physical energy; it also includes psychological, emotional, and spiritual energy.

This bathtub of life-energy is part of you yet separate from you. It is separate and (not part of you) because you did not give yourself life, thus your life and the energy that is refilled daily is a gift, and at the same time it is part of you because you have access to this life-energy and free choice on how to use it.

PART 1

The Liar Side of the Model

Let us begin with the bad news first. I call this The Liar Side of the Model. It is also known as the unbalanced, unnatural, and isolated side of the model. To make it easy, I will refer to it as the unbalanced side of the model. A friend of mine asked me to put an advisory here: This section may shock you; it is OK if it does. Hang in there and be present and learn what you can. The balanced side is coming next.

3. False image

Your ego provides the beliefs, "I am not good enough as I am, with all my faults, failures, flaws, and feebleness."

"I am nothing" and "I am not OK" are the root and trunk of The Liar's Tree. The ego bombards us with messages that reinforce this lie. What do we do? We protect ourselves. We create a diversion, a mirage for others, an image of ourselves that is not really who we are. What this image looks like depends on the threats that surround us at the time, but it will typically be one of three types: Inferiority, Superiority, and Please Validate Me.

> *Authenticity is being without thinking, speaking from the heart, not editing oneself to suit anyone or anything. When our voice rings true, it is our soul that speaks, our true authentic self.*
>
> —Lucy Vignola

Whatever lie you choose to support will generate a false image. This false image is anything that you project that is not who you truly are. Notice the incredible amount of energy that is consumed in maintaining the false

Get off Your High Horse and Walk.

> *No one man can, for any considerable time, wear one face to himself, and another to the multitude, without finally getting bewildered as to which is the true one."*
>
> —Hawthorne

image. You are consuming vital life energy to support a lie. Notice the holes in the balloon; this balloon is not authentic and by its nature is flawed. We can experience this drain as physical, emotional, psychological, or spiritual depletion.

When was the last time that you felt completely drained and tapped, emotionally, psychologically, or spiritually? Try to identify the events that surrounded the depletion. Were you being true to yourself and to the others involved, or was a false image involved?

The Liar Side of the Model

Energy contraction and expansion model

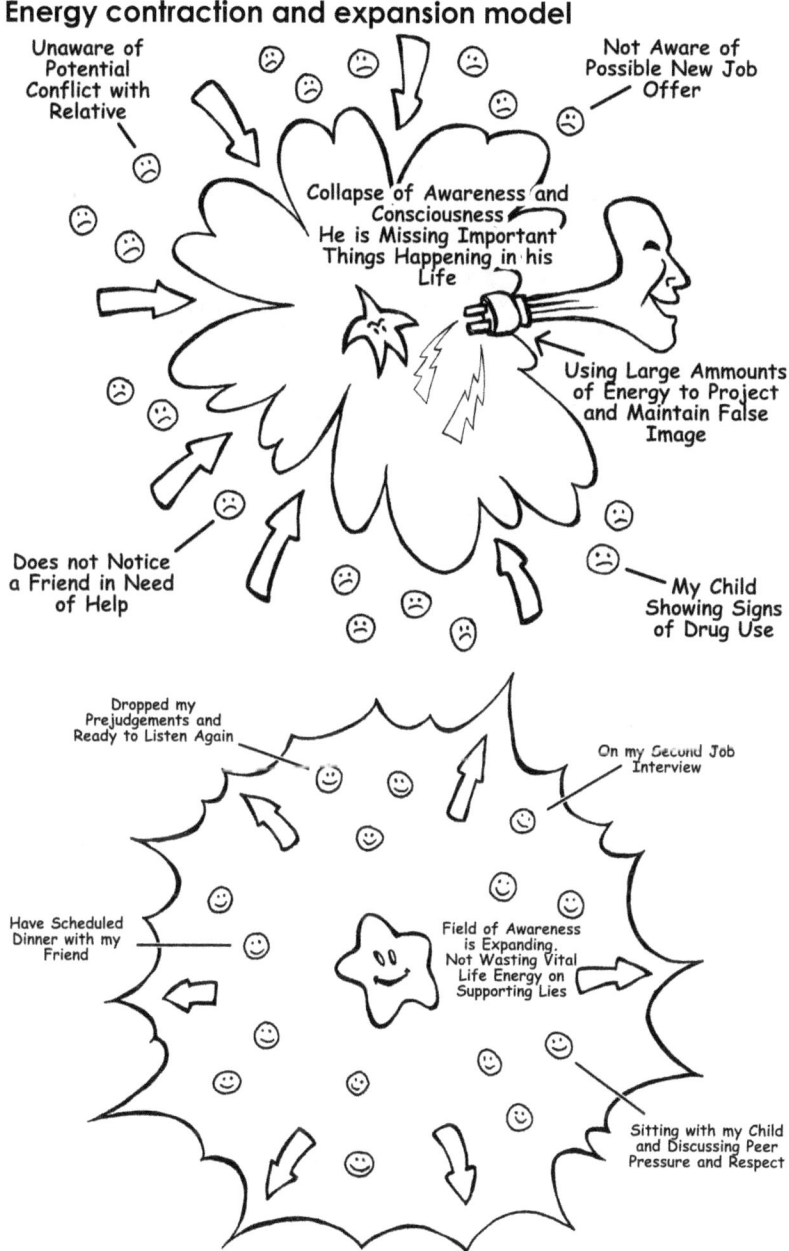

Get off Your High Horse and Walk.

Do you see how your energy expands and contracts corresponding to whether or not you are projecting a false image? It may be helpful to see yourself as a radio transmitter. If you are busy projecting a false image of yourself, then you are, in effect, transmitting at a lower emotional frequency (such as fear, jealousy, hatred, apathy, etc.), which cannot support a large energy field of consciousness, so it collapses around you. Notice what happens to important and vital events around you when your conscious energy field has collapsed. You lose perspective, and your senses become dull, your ability to see and hear become hampered by your ego self-centric focus. You are no longer aware that someone may need your help, or you miss the signs of someone who would like to hire you for a new position, etc.

> *If you feel Love, Express Love, no matter what.*
> —Jacek Skrzypczynski

When you have no need to project and defend a false image of yourself you begin to transmit higher emotional frequencies (such as compassion, love, joy, empathy, etc.) and as a result your conscious energy field begins to naturally expand where you can sense important vital events unfolding in your life. Your senses become acute (heightened), you gain other perspectives. Your focus is not on your navel (bellybutton), you are plugged into and aware of others and God/universe. You may have heard others refer to this as a spiritual field. I believe this to be the same thing.

4. Taking the stage (interaction with your false image)

Taking the stage in real life is "busy" business. There is a plot that needs to be followed; there are costume changes, different masks to project, and you have to keep up with all the other actors and make sure that the audience has a convincing show.

It is the same busy work when you take the stage inside yourself. You have something to prove, explain, justify, hide, protect, and defend. You have a lot to lose. Failure to act convincingly will reveal you as the fraud that you have already agreed to play. This is sufficient motivation to make your act convincing to others and especially to yourself. You know well that right after the performance, you will be required to justify your act.

When you are on stage, you feel alone. After all, you are playing a role that is not really yours, and everyone is watching your performance.

5. Personal Judge and Stage Manager: Your ego

The ego's main job is to make sure that you take the stage. After that, most of its work is done. When you are on stage, you play your role and wear a mask for everyone to see. It is difficult to leave the stage, because if you do, everyone will see you as a fraud. The fact that you have taken the stage means that you are already defending a lie or an image of yourself that is not true.

> *As we express our gratitude, we must never forget that the highest appreciation is not to utter words, but to live by them.*
>
> —John F. Kennedy

The ego stands behind the stage, ready to hand you a big fat check of validation for your successful performance. If you fail on stage or your conscience gets in the way, your ego is equally prepared to judge your lack of motivation to act. Your ego has tools such as guilt, shame, apathy, and its prize of prizes, fear.

Professional actors require time and energy in preparing to become the character they play. You and I do not require this preparation, nor do we need to rehearse. The ego is two steps ahead of us and has prepared everything for us.

I am going to have a bit of fun and refer to my ego as "Sly." Sly makes a wonderful Stage Manager, as he wants to make performance easy for me so that I do not have to think. All I need to do is to be reactionary, wear the appropriate mask, and play the appropriate role.

> *Humor is mankind's greatest blessing.*
> —Mark Twain

Sly cares about everything I think and is careful to control what I feel. He wants to ensure that I have a steady diet of fear. He carefully stokes the fire of invalidation, ensuring that I do not feel OK as I am, making it necessary to look for validation outside myself.

Your ego has three jobs:
- To serve as a catalyst of inadequacy, by convincing you that you are not OK as you are, alone, vulnerable, and weak, and you need to be protected from the outside world.
- To be the most efficient Stage Manager you will ever know. It will justify your actions and behaviors as needed, all in the name of "protecting you from others."
- To play the role of your Personal Judge. It will punish you, using anger, blame, or guilt if you get cold feet or act from conscience. It will do whatever it takes to make sure that you take the stage.

The unbalanced stage offers three types of acting, and you are familiar with them: "I am superior," "I am inferior," and "Please validate me."

6. **Acting from the stage**
The ego tries to hide the fact that people have built-in lie detectors. They can often detect whether someone is being honest. Wanting to believe that our lies go unde-

tected, or believing that our audience does not have these detectors, are ways to deceive ourselves. Most everyone is willing to play the game of deceit and not bust you, because they are doing the same thing, hoping that you will not bust them. If someone questions your motivations while you are on stage, projecting your false image, you may become defensive and reactionary (I do).

> *If I had no sense of humor, I would long ago have committed suicide.*
>
> —Mohandas Gandhi

You may have noticed that your decision-making capacity is hampered, because while "acting," you are in a contracted state. Your on-stage interaction with others will focus your energy on convincing others that you "appear authentic." This will explain why you have little energy available for creativity. Your interactions with others will be sterile and unimaginative (imagine the impact this has on the business world). You will need to lie in order to defend a lie, which requires more and more energy.

The saying "What goes around comes around" demonstrates that what you put out is what you eventually get back. When you are interacting with an angry person, the response you generate will typically be anger. You are a mirror of aggression. "Manifesting like energies" is true for both positive and negative energy.

The stage is located on the unbalanced, unnatural, and forced side of the model. What does this mean to you while you are on stage? More energy consumption! It means that you have to "act" to prove to others that you are balanced when you are not.

7. Cloud of fear

Defending something that is false has consequences. By doing so, you create toxic by-products. Much like the

CO_2 produced by burning fossil fuels, a cloud of fear and mistrust is produced when you try to justify a false image.

Each time you take the stage wearing a mask, you become more obscure. It's like a cheap science fiction movie come true! The uneasiness comes from the disharmony of not knowing yourself.

> *What usually has the strongest psychic effect on the child is the life which the parents have not lived*
> —Carl Jung

The more you repeat this lie, protecting your self-image, the thicker this cloud becomes, and the more you start to believe that the created image is truly you. As long as you continue to defend the lie "*I* am not good enough as I am," fear will continue to guide your actions. Your Personal Judge will have power over you, and you will continue to protect something that is false.

8. Polluting your pure life gift

When a cloud becomes condensed enough, precipitation is possible. Similar to acid rain, the cloud of fear begins to influence and pollute your pure life gift. Fear, emptiness, mistrust, and failure further justify the idea that "I am less than, more than, or not OK as I am."

The more cycles you make through the negative side of the model, the more acid rain is produced and the more tainted your life energy becomes.

You do not have any direct input on your pure life gift of energy, but you can influence it in a negative way by choosing to live in fear and mistrust. The more poisoned your life energy becomes, the less you will be able to access your sense of humor and creativity. Watch for these signs.

A dump or a piggy bank?

Imagine that you collect twenty-four apples from a tree, and go to an area where people are starving. You place the apples near a group of hungry children, untie the bag, and walk away. Then imagine going to a farm and placing a bag on the ground under the backside of a horse. After the horse completes his business, you take the horse waste to a busy sidewalk of the city, open the bag, and walk away.

In these two scenarios, what you leave behind is quite different. I am not referring to the apples or the horse manure: I am referring to your lasting impact on the people.

Your impact is powerful, whether it is positive or negative. I guarantee you the resentment of the people on the busy sidewalk who step in the horse manure, as well as the gratitude from the children, will live on and influence others.

> *You should really learn how to climb down a tree before you climb up.*
>
> —Jim Suiter

The bag of manure on the sidewalk is a "dump" situation (people are constricting), while the bag of apples creates a "piggy bank" situation (people become open and happy).

Whenever you project a false image or take the stage, you are investing in a "dump" that will constrict and influence others. Even if your false image is not aggressive, the fact that your authentic self is not present creates a "dump" situation. On the other hand, when you are present and allowing yourself to be authentic, you create a "piggy bank" where your presence and actions will have a positive influence.

PART 2

The Balanced Side of the Model

"To be, or not to be: that is the question."

—Shakespeare

The balanced side of the model consists of your essence (your authentic self), a direct connection to God–Universe, and a direct connection with other people and nature. I do not have anything to teach you here, because everything here is in your experiential level. You already know this place.

> *"If you do not tell the truth about yourself, you cannot tell it about other people."*
> —Virginia Woolf

Perhaps it has been a long while since you have been here. You can do nothing to understand it with your head. It would be like the ocean trying to understand the concept of wet or like trying to explain "wet" to a person who has never touched water. You can use many words, but at the end of the day, no one will understand you. Give a person a bucket of water and let him or her experience what wet is. The balanced side of the model is about *experience*.

The difference between the unbalanced side and the balanced side is that there is absolutely nothing you can do to arrive at your authentic self. It is exactly the opposite of doing. It is about allowing. Your essence is a natural place that you gravitate to when there is nothing stopping you. Being caught up in a tangled web of lies, defending your false self-image, and performing on stage all prevent you from accessing your place of authenticity. It's a matter of becoming aware of what takes you away from your essence and prevents you from returning.

Think of the times when you felt most at home inside of yourself—how did you get there? What did you do? Did it feel natural to you? You allowed yourself, and it was probably something you didn't even consider doing. It just happened.

> *Authenticity is lifting the lid and experiencing the essence of who we are. Making "authenticity" a life style that includes any fear and aliveness that comes along with it.*
> —Neta Kafri

The terms "authentic side," "essential side," "balanced side," and "natural side" of the model all refer to the same thing; the terms are used interchangeably.

You will also hear me refer to the left side of the model as "the liar's side," "the unbalanced side," and "the unnatural side."

The balanced side has the full range of your emotions available, whereas the unbalanced side restricts and distorts your emotions, ensuring that you stay locked in the liar's cycle.

The balanced side does not mean a life without problems. It is a matter of who is in charge of your life: your ego and the image that you created or your authentic self.

9. Your pure life gift

The balanced side of the model starts from the pure gift of life. You will see that this gift is and at the same time is not part of you. You did nothing to earn it. The gifts of life and energy are available to you every day when you wake up. Notice the small amount of energy that is feeding into your essence. Your essence can be seen as a perfect sphere that does not contain holes, because it is your truth.

What happens to this life energy bathtub when your essence does not require much to sustain itself and you are not wasting precious energy maintaining lies? This is the coolest part of the model. The energy becomes available for you to use and create with. The greatest uses of this vital life bathtub of energy are creating, loving, and learning. Michelangelo, Leonardo da Vinci, Mozart, Newton, Rembrandt, Socrates, Plato, Mother Teresa, Lao Tzu, and Shakespeare all required incredible amounts of energy to pursue their passions. They had energy available to them, because they were not wasting it on false images of themselves. They created great works by being connected to something bigger from the inside. Did they fit in to society? Did they find it important to fit in? In which ways did they stand out?

> *Truth is what stands the test of experience.*
> —Albert Einstein

Contemporaries who did not appreciate their unorthodox approaches to life criticized the above-mentioned people. They struggled with their shadows (their unbalanced side) as well. The difference is that the unbalanced side of the model covers up their shadows, whereas the balanced side of the model confronts the shadows with their truths.

People with a passion choose to reject many parts of "normal" life and focus their energies on their passion. This is the reason why many people see them as "strange and different."

10. Your authentic self or essence

I found it helpful to describe this place as an area of experiential expansion. Some may refer to this as their inner child (who has the awe and excitement for learning). It is your place of great understanding and wisdom. It is here where you have a direct wire, a connection, with the greater being, God, universal love, and all things on this earth. You have a sense of connectedness while you are at home in your authentic self.

This is the place of your essence, it's the place of your truths, it is your expansion as a human, it is the "it," and returning to "it" is the experience of "returning home."

In your essence, you will find your personal truth. Note that this is not "*the*" truth; rather, it is "*your*" truth. Your personal truth is tied to and depends on the common universal truth (God-Universe). This means that your personal truth is growing and learning as you do. Isn't that neat? As it does, the expression of your truth will constantly change, adjusting itself in reference to the bigger truth. It would not be possible without the fertilizer of humility where we can be open to learn and grow our truth.

> *Be your authentic self. Your authentic self is who you are when you have no fear of judgment, or before the world starts pushing you around and telling you who you're supposed to be.*
>
> —Dr. Phil

From your truth, you find a purpose in life that is fueled by passion. Some people may know this as a calling, destiny, or their life's quest.

Every living thing on this earth has its own movement or expression of itself. The same goes for your truth. Once you are in touch with it, it naturally wants to express itself. The catalyst for this expression is your passion. True passion is a deep desire to create from what is discovered in your essential truth. Great symphonies, paintings, statues, poetry, and scientific breakthroughs are all passion in action.

Where does inspiration come from?

It is impossible for people to be inspired when they are caught on the lying side of the model. Inspiration taps into and accesses every living thing on earth and God-Universe. You can see now why it is so important for great artists, thinkers, and philosophers to be at home in their authenticity. They are creating from something much bigger than themselves. This is why you hear authors say that they are surprised by what they see on the pages and, from artists, how paintbrushes take on their own life. All who experience this in their work recognize the bigger truth in its individual expression.

Have you ever heard a "little voice" or felt a "funny feeling" trying to tell you something? It is your intuition. Your intuition is a part of communication that is ancient. Every living thing knows how to communicate on this level. You know how to speak this language, but you may have become rusty at using it.

> *Truth is by nature self-evident. As soon as you remove the cobwebs of ignorance that surround it, it shines clear.*
> —Mohandas Gandhi

This voice speaks clearest when you are present in your essence; it has a clarity and a quality of "OK-ness" that is detached from drama.

The ancient language

Imagine that you were exploring space, and you came across an unexplored planet, and on this planet, you found a fascinating device of alien technology.

You started to investigate this alien device, and you found that it had extraordinary powers beyond your comprehension. You discovered that this device could communicate with you in a way that it bypassed language or rationality; it talked directly to your essence. It used a language that we can easily understand, because it communicated through our ancient language. It directly connected with the experiences, emotions, feelings, and concepts that we could understand, similar to the way we do when we are dreaming. We were able to discover and know another universe, another life form, and all the learning and growth it had to offer us. It wasn't long until we started to name, judge and scrutinize the validity of this device. How could we trust something that we couldn't understand or put into words? Soon galaxy exploration committees grew fearful and decided that the device was not to be trusted. It was not a valid way to communicate and was labeled and stored away for future studies.

A bit of a stretch? The point is that when we are stuck on the liar side of the model, we lose understanding and possibilities, because we do not trust the knowing and essential part of ourselves. We can do it, but we cannot understand it. It defies our rational capabilities because it is bigger than reason. It also illustrates our overwhelming need to have things safely labeled and categorized. It is difficult and uncomfortable for us to trust anything outside of our comprehension. That is exactly what we're doing here: trusting that place where words are nonexistent.

> *He who knows nothing is closer to the truth than he whose mind is filled with falsehoods and errors.*
>
> —Thomas Jefferson

What is our essence? How can we relate to the world in this way without words?

Your essence is where your truth lives.

Many people living on the unbalanced side of the model pursue freedom and happiness to fulfill their lives, only to have happiness and the sense of freedom disperse like a cloud of vapor when they discover that they are prisoners of self-deceit. They disappear because freedom and happiness are experiences. They cannot be pursued and achieved. They are not available as ends in themselves. Your ego wants you to believe that they can be sought and won like a prize. The reality is that they don't exist on the unbalanced side at all.

Happiness and freedom exist on the balanced side of the model; they are by-products of living your truth. You couldn't keep them away if you tried. This is the big payoff for returning to your authenticity.

Compare the two models side by side, and you will see how the natural model is less complicated. What does this say about us when we are being authentic? Are we by nature simple or complicated? If you answer complex (notice what side of the model this answer comes from), perhaps the alternative is becoming something more simple.

11. Interaction with the world

The quality of interaction with the world is different from the lying side of the model. There is nothing to protect or hide from others. This gives communication from your authentic essence a level of quality and of receptivity. The same law of attraction is in play. You generate a similar "receptive response" from the world.

> *Do not think that love, in order to be genuine, has to be extraordinary.*
>
> —Mother Theresa

Notice that there is a cable or cord connecting your essence to the world. Likewise, you will see a cable connecting God-Universe to your essence. Your spirituality (your relationship to your higher power) becomes healthy and balanced. As a result you are present, aware, and feel no need to prove yourself because you feel "OK" with who you are.

The idea "I am not alone, and I am connected to others" will impact your actions, and your actions will impact who you are connected to. You will begin to notice the responsibility you have directly and indirectly to other humans and the planet we live on.

You start to notice yourself in other people.

A man named John Bradford was burned at the stake at age forty-five by Queen Mary (also known as "Bloody Mary"). Bradford 's famous saying came from watching criminals being led to their executions. He said, "There but for the grace of God go I." This meant that he saw himself in the prisoners, and only the circumstances separated him from the prisoners. In the end, there was no difference, for he was also led off to execution.

When we understand this, we start to treat everyone with more respect.

I am sure that you can look around at the people you know and identify individuals who have that direct cord connecting them to others. They are not easy to miss. These people make healthy friends and companions.

> *Who we are looking for is who is looking.*
> —Francis of Assisi

Our actions are important as we are becoming who we are. We are making deposits in the piggy bank of humanity. Nothing is too small, and everything adds. Once we become aware that what we create will last forever, it becomes a motivation in itself to contribute to something bigger. Imagine that simply allowing ourselves to be authentic is creating a better world. Wow!

Once we have created it, "what we have created" will last forever (piggy bank), and then we can create and build further.

Chapter Summary
- There is something that is bigger than you (God-Universe).
- The pure life gift is yours, and it's not. You're alive, so choose wisely.
- As a simple law of physics, we work with quantifiable amounts of energy. How we use our energy impacts everything in our lives. Focusing our energy in projecting false images decreases our energy field. Many important events in our lives can go unnoticed and unchecked, because our awareness has decreased.

- When our energy is not being used to support a false image of ourselves, our energy naturally expands, giving us awareness of vital happenings.
- The dump or the piggy bank is your choice. Everything you do or do not do will have a lasting residual effect. Negative actions against others or yourself will add to the collective dump, whereas positive actions and creativity toward others, the world, or yourself add to the collective piggy bank.

The Liar Side of the Model

False image: Anything that you project that is not truly you.

Taking the stage: Putting on a mask and playing the roles given to you. Show to everyone that you are worthwhile.

Stage Manager and Personal Judge: Your ego: Ready to validate your performance or pound you over the head for failing to convince others of your act.

> *Authenticity is the natural ability to be oneself without fear of conformity, while keeping the balance between your personal values and the culture you live in...*
>
> —Harry Sargent

Acting from the stage: We will manifest the same type (frequency) of energy we use to defend our false self-image. Once we take the stage it is very difficult to turn back.

Cloud of fear: Using vital life energy to defend a false image, produces a toxic byproduct of fear.

Polluting your life gift: When the cloud of fear becomes thick and produces a lasting toxic residue that begins to taint color, we begin to pollute our precious life gift. This results in us beginning to believe in the lies that we created.

The Balanced Side of the Model

Pure life gift: You already know this place by your experience.

> *This above all:*
> *To thine own self be true,*
> *And it must follow, as the night the day,*
> *Thou canst not then be false to any man.*
> —Hamlet, Shakespeare

Your authentic self (essence): This is 50 percent yours, and 50 percent gift (refillable in twenty-four-hour cycles). Big objective toward authenticity is this day, and remaining conscious of your life at all times.

Ancient language: Before humanity developed the words to communicate, it fits that there was an ancient language in place, comprised of essence and intuition. This language is congruent in nature, experienced and communicated the same way we use it today. We need to relearn how to use and trust this vital way of communicating.

Interaction with the world and God-Universe: The authentic person has a direct connection to the world. Communication has a receptive quality to it. The world, likewise, is receptive to the authentic person due to the law of attraction. Like energy seeks like energy.

When people live at their essence, there is an understanding that "I am OK as I am." There is no need to project any image. The world recognizes the authenticity by the use of the ancient language. Spirituality becomes healthy and is motivated out of love and respect rather than guilt and shame.

CHAPTER 8:

On The Shoulders Of Giants

I recently visited with a great physicist, Dr. Jose Alberto Lobo, who lives in Barcelona. We talked about the people who are adding to the concept of consciousness. He shared a quote best known by Isaac Newton, who was asked how he could see so far in his theories. Newton said, "We are like dwarves sitting on the shoulders of giants. We see more and things that are more distant than they did, not because our sight is superior or because we are taller than they, but because they raise us up, and by their great stature, add to ours."

> *"Trust is the great simplifier. If people in business told the truth, 80 to 90 percent of their problems would disappear."*
>
> —Will Schutz

In the light of collective consciousness, when we create something that someone else has contributed to, it means that we're contributing to a universal piggy bank. Once something is created, it will last forever and be available to other strange and wonderful people like ourselves.

This book is adding to those shoulders.

As you can see by the people who have contributed quotes on authenticity, the foundation that I'm building on is the shoulders of these individuals.

The following segment from the *Tao Te Ching* was written in about the third or fourth century BC. It has to do with "coming home."

Accept and you become whole,
Bend and you straighten,
Empty and you fill,

Decay and you renew,
Want and you acquire,
Fulfill and you become confused.

The sage accepts the world
As the world accepts the Way;
He does not display himself, so is clearly seen,
Does not justify himself, so is recognized,
Does not boast, so is credited,
Does not pride himself, so endures,
Does not contend, so none contend against him.

The ancients said, "Accept and you become whole,"
Once whole, the world is as your home.

The ancient Greeks equated beauty with balance. They sought balance, for in balance was perfection. If we want to see this in action, we have to back up to gain a bigger perspective. We need to take into consideration the polarities of life in order to find balance. Imagine yourself walking on a tightrope through your life, your hands outstretched, each step wobbly and insecure, as you move. Is that beauty? To me, it's not. It sounds like a stressful way of living.

> *Live as if you were to die tomorrow. Learn as if you were to live forever.*
> —Mohandas Gandhi

Polarities exist in all things—day into night, morning into evening, summer and winter, autumn and spring, rage and love. There is a time for everything. There is a time to experience the polarities, and by understanding this, we ensure the possibility of balance.

There are no tightropes between the polarities. There is a time to experience the polarities, and balance comes with discovering how to live between them in harmony. This is beauty.

Energy differences between the models

Notice the great amount of energy that is required to maintain a false image. Compare that to the natural side of the model. Remember that you do not have to spend energy trying to become who you already are.

Imagine that you cut out the lies that have been consuming your energy and attention. You then naturally gravitate to authentic self. If your life energy bathtub remains full, how will you use it? Don't worry; you will never have to answer that question. When you are on the balanced, natural side of the model, things become clear, and your energy field expands (recall the contraction-expansion illustration). You notice important happenings, whereas before you did not notice them. It is not a question of how best to use this energy. It is relaxing into something that is already familiar and trusting your intuition to guide you.

People throughout history have put these ideas to good use.

> *"If you are not prepared to resign or be fired for what you believe in, then you are not a worker, let alone a professional. You are a slave."*
>
> —Howard Gardner

Chapter Summary

- As Newton stated, we stand on the shoulders of giants, building on the knowledge and creativity of those who came before us. The authentic person in his or her essence is by nature receptive and willing to learn from others, knowing that personal truth is not "*the*" truth. The Greeks found beauty in balance. We need the polarities of life as well as our own experience to live the beauty of balance.
- Notice the energy (on the unbalanced side of the model) used in maintaining a false image, and compare it to the balanced side of the model, where you do not have to spend energy trying to become who you already are.

CHAPTER 9:

How Does This Model Show Up In Our Lives?

*"This above all:
to thine own self be true,
and it must follow, as the night the day,
thou canst not then be false to any man."*

—Shakespeare

There is little difference between personal lies and professional lies. Think of your own experience in dealing with others in the business world. Someone decided that when you entered the office or began your business day, you stopped being human and magically transformed into a businessperson.

> *The kingdom of Heaven is within you... Seek first the kingdom of Heaven and all things will be added unto you.*
>
> —Jesus Christ

You have a defined role and function to follow. You have meetings, quotas, deadlines, and sales projections to meet. You do this by adopting your company's mission statement as your own and saying to yourself, "I will now project a professional image. This image that you see is not really who I am. I have a new set of priorities to follow. If I make my quota, if I make my projected sales, if I land a new client, I am seen as valuable, and I am recognized professionally as being OK."

I have had many experiences with professionals of this type. Many people are willing to forget who they are and slip into a professional and lesser image of themselves. There is a sense that "I do what I need to do in order to be accepted, and thus, successful in the business," and that usually includes lying. This is what happens when you project an image that is not you. It does not have anything to do with how others see you. It has everything to do with how you are not showing up!

You can read people. You have always been able to. You know when they're telling you the truth and when they're holding something back. It's time to stop playing idiot, take ownership of your built-in lie detector, and use it! Trusting your capabilities without judging yourself or others is the key. This lie detector works both ways, as other people have the same capability to detect honesty and deception. If there is truth to what you say and who you project, how will this impact future business? Imagine that you had no hidden agenda, no deceptions, and no pressure in your business dealings to present a false image. What kind of an impact would that make?

> *"Authenticity is acting in alignment with one's deep values and linking inner work with outer work to have consistently positive impact on people and situations".*
> —Okokon Udo

Imagine that you work in a poisonous business environment where people do not talk to each other or trust each other. There is a high sense of competition, and success is rare, because limited resources are not shared with other departments. Imagine that you are having a business meeting and the supervisor asks, "Why are we not meeting our projections?" Everyone at the table is aware of the answer but afraid to speak it. They remain silent. (This is an example of "Prostitutes Are Us").

Let's imagine the same situation in a different way. When you joined this company, you made the decision to always be yourself, no matter what position or status you had. Imagine that you are transferred into this poisonous department. You're sitting in the meeting where your boss is asking, "Why are we not meeting our projections?" You then stand up (you read the space and the energy of the room) and say your truth as you see it without any judgment or blame. >The room is silent<

Putting the truth on the line
Do not try this at home, unless it is your truth!
A good friend of mine works as an information technology specialist at a major corporation in Omaha, Nebraska. He supported over three hundred people and was very busy most of the time. He spent most of his time "putting out fires," and the problem was that there was only one of him. At the end of the day, he was tired and frustrated.

> *Be who you are and say what you feel because those who mind don't matter and those who matter don't mind.*
> —Dr. Seuss
> (1904 - 1991)

This man truly cared about the people he was supporting so much so that he refused to lie to them. When something went wrong with the equipment or a situation, he told them the truth, even if the truth shed light on his own department's shortcomings.

As in all large corporations, there is a constant tug of war for finances. One day, he heard that the company was pulling the funding for the additional support that had been promised and that it was increasing the number of people that he supported by two hundred.

He appealed to his manager, who said she could do nothing. He went to his supervisor and again heard, "There is nothing I can do." He wrote a letter and sent it to the managers, supervisors, the vice president, and the president of the company. He was prepared to be fired by letting the truth be known about the impact the cut would have on the people he supported. That evening, he sent the letter.

Get off Your High Horse and Walk.

The next day, all hell broke loose. He was told, "This is your last day here." His supervisor screamed in his face, his veins pulsing in his forehead, saying, "You had no right to write and send this letter!"

I could tell you that the man was fired for standing up for what he believed was truthful, but that would be a lie. The supervisor who threatened him was fired. My friend had an audience with the executive vice president and the president to explain the situation as it really was. As a result, my friend was promoted.

> *You may make a jewelry flower out of gold and rubys and emeralds, but it will not have fragrance.*
> —Mevlana Rumi
> (1207 - 1273)

Why wasn't he fired, as everyone expected? Why in the world was he promoted? Why did his letter have such impact? This takes us back to that internal truths/lie detector that we all have. The president and vice presidents of his company detected truths through his letter and actions. I asked my friend, "What made you so courageous to write this letter?" He answered, "I cared about the people who I support and I remember consciously accepting personal responsibility for this letter before I pressed the send key."

This is an example of that direct cable connection to the world on the balance side the model. My friend gained strength through that direct cable connection that he had to others that he was supporting. Their discomfort and corporate indifference added strength to his words and reinforced his actions.

The accident

Some things in life drop-kick us into our life gift energy. Life and death situations usually do the trick.

My wife and I live in Barcelona, and we have a parking space several levels below ground. I was taking my son to school and dropping my wife off at the train station. On the way down in the elevator, I heard a huge crash that I dismissed as construction of some type. As we arrived at the car, we heard a haunting yell that echoed in the garage. My actions surprised me. I set out in search of the yelling. I wanted to dismiss it as a child playing games or yelling to get attention from his parents, but I instinctually knew that this was a plea for help.

We drove to the level above us and saw a car slammed into a stone wall and a lady crying and yelling. I saw a total transformation in my wife, myself, and my son. When we learned that the yelling was real, our "real selves" responded. I witnessed how the best in us emerges when we are dealing with life's pure gift.

> "No legacy is so rich as honesty."
> —Shakespeare

We were first on the scene and provided assistance. At first look, this woman was not terribly injured. The car was severely smashed, and the airbags deployed. She was by the driver's door, bracing herself against the car with her weight on one leg. She handed my wife a phone and asked her to call her husband and tell him where she was and what had happened. We left the garage to get mobile reception and called the fire department and an ambulance. We went back into the garage, and more people had come to assist. Things looked like they were in hand, so we went on our way. The lady thanked us for assisting her.

In the car, there was a palpable change in all of us. We were all touched by the authentic drama of an emergency situation; it wiped away insignificant matters and replaced them with a sense of connection to that life gift bathtub. We all commented on it.

After dropping off my wife and son, I returned to the garage and found the lady in a worse condition. The ambulance had not arrived, but her husband was at her side. The way that he held his wife, looked at her, and offered words of comfort were a direct connection from his essence to her essence. Those standing around were able to experience it and understand it on a level so deep that there were no words. This is what love is: a true connection of essence.

If we can stay connected to our pure life gift energy, we naturally gravitate to our authentic selves. Many people make the error of saying, "Who am I?" This engages the mind, and your ego intercepts and is all too happy to answer it for you. Try simply saying, "I am alive!" This bypasses your mind and directly transports you to your life gift bathtub. You are naturally drawn to your authentic self.

> *Speak your ***** truth*
> —Suzanne Dahlerus

Chapter Summary

- When living on the liar's side of the model, you are a spineless wimp in the workplace. You have low self-confidence and fear of reprisal. You empower competition, and you are reluctant to speak your truth. People have the same built-in lie detector that you do, and they are able to detect whether you present honesty or deception.
- Stand up for your truth, putting it on the line, and accept personal responsibility for your actions.
- Life-and-death situations have a way of drop-kicking you directly to your vital life gift. Your vital life gift acts as a sifter, separating important events from the garbage.

CHAPTER 10:

How Do We Get Unstuck From The Stickiness?

When you are stuck in the liar's side of the model, throwing mud everywhere, your tires spinning around and around, you are stuck. It may appear from the outside as if you are doing a lot, but if you back off to gain prospective, you see (and feel) that you are not moving. When you are reactive and hiding from yourself, you are stagnant. You already know how you react in confrontations and avoid decision making.

> *We shall not cease from exploration*
> *And the end of all our exploring*
> *Will be to arrive where we started*
> *And know the place for the first time.*
>
> —T. S. Eliot

You have a completely different set of tools available when you are on the right side of the model. On the liar's side, fear motivates you, while the balanced side has your truth to serve you as your guide. You also have a wonderful tool called your imagination. Much like our functioning body parts, we take our imagination for granted and most likely put it aside in childhood.

How can we break down the walls or, rather, allow them to fall?

Laughing at yourself

I have come to believe that humor is the most divine and Godlike quality. Whenever I'm able to really laugh, I feel right. If I cannot laugh, I am in deep doo-doo.

The idea is not to take yourself so seriously. Adopting and cultivating a sense of humor will counterbalance rigidity and resistance that keeps you from making progress. It is impossible to be able to laugh at yourself in a lighthearted way and maintain rigidity. Put it to the test.

Natural failure

If you have told yourself that "failure is not an option," you are already working against nature. Nature learns through failure. Humans are the only animal that will return to a bad situation. Take lion cubs for example. They understand their limits. They learn how to be successful with a little bite from their mother here and a mouse escaping from their paws there. They don't run from failure, neither do they look for it; they learn from it. There is discomfort in being bitten and frustration when the mouse escapes. The lion cub is able to let go immediately, because he is always present, while humans are not!

> *That inner voice has both gentleness and clarity. So to get to authenticity, you really keep going down to the bone, to the honesty, and the inevitability of something.*
>
> —Meredith Monk

Our ego masks failures from us, using denial, anger, or shame. We must learn from failure and accept it as a natural part of our lives.

You can see the importance of a healthy sense of humor in the face of failure. This alone will set you free to learn and grow without all that unnecessary fear of failing. Imagine how brave you would become if you consciously allowed yourself to be able to fail. How often has fear of failure held you back?

It's not all your ego's fault after all

Your ego is the part that stepped up to bat because of your lack of presence. You most likely stepped down because you listened to the lies around you, and you bought into the fears that you are nothing and not OK as you are. Your ego believes that it is really *you*.

The next time you feel yourself tightening up, contracting, or resisting, try using your imagination and humor.

Give your ego a name. It doesn't matter what you call it, and I suggest something fun. You can give it the image that you want as well. This way you will easily be able to identify what until now has been invisible.

I have given my ego (Stage Manager/Personal Judge) the name of Big Boy. I tell it something like this:

"Hey, Big Boy, I want you to see that I have my hand open to you. In no way do I wish to fight you. You would wipe me out, like you usually do. On the contrary, I want to thank you. I have been asleep for many years, but I'm awake again. I know you have struggled all these years to give me an identity and to keep me safe. Thank you for that. I invite you to come back home and reintegrate into me. I want to let you know that I am here, there is nothing to fear, I am patient, and my hand is open to you. I see what you're trying to do. I understand that you're trying to stop me from crossing a line of security. I know you are doing this to keep me from getting hurt. I want you to know that I have consciously decided to cross this line in order to be authentic. Yes, I feel afraid to cross that line. I want you to know that this is a conscious decision, and so I invite you to step down and let me pass."

Use the words of your choosing. Notice that this is like a conversation between old friends, with someone you know well and you have confidence in. Notice the lack of confrontation. I acknowledge the functions the ego plays

> *The accusation that we've lost our soul resonates with a very modern concern about authenticity.*
>
> —Patricia Hewitt

as Stage Manager/Personal Judge. I follow up with an invitation and a nonthreatening gesture of my intention to step back into authenticity.

The Prodigal Son

This story can be found in the Christian Bible. It is a story of unconditional love that a father had for his child. This quote is lengthy so I will give you the "Slade" version.

> *Is devotion to others a cover for the hungers and the needs of the self, of which one is ashamed? I was always ashamed to take. So I gave. It was not a virtue. It was a disguise.*
> —Anaïs Nin (1903 - 1977)

There once was a man who had two sons. One day his youngest son approached him and said, "Father, I want you to sell everything that is coming to me for my inheritance. So his father sadly and reluctantly sold half of everything and gave the money to his youngest son and off he went to a distant land and began to spend his money on wild and wasteful living. As time passed, an economic crisis fell across the land. Soon afterward, this boy exhausted all of his wealth and found himself on the street starving. All of his friends abandoned him, leaving him alone and helpless. He eventually found a job feeding pigs, and was so hungry that he wanted to eat the slop that he was feeding the pigs. And that's when he came to his senses (awareness, became conscious) and saw that he was in a situation of almost starving to death, whereas his father's servants had plenty more than enough to eat.

He thought, I will go to him and plead with him to take me on as one of his servants, and so he set off.

Meanwhile, his father, day after day, kept a vigil in hopes that one day his son would return. While he was still a ways off, his father recognized him and ran as fast as his old legs could take him toward his son. When his son caught sight of his father running toward him he yelled, "Father, I have sinned against you and I have sinned against God. I am no longer worthy to be called your son. The father plowed into him, hugged him, and said, "Enough! You are my son." He started issuing orders to the servants to get some clothes for the boy and shoes for his feet. "Go kill the fatted calf, set up for a fiesta, we are going to have a feast because my boy, who was lost, is found; who was once dead, is now alive."

Now, his older brother on his way in from a hard day in the fields heard the music and discovered from one of the servants that his brother had returned home and his father was celebrating. Anger flared in the older brother and he refused to go in. His father came out, pleading for him to join the celebration. "Are you kidding? My brother comes skipping home after living a life of self-deception and dumping half of his fortune on prostitutes and riotous living and you reward him with a fiesta? What in the heck is this? Look, I have been with you all of these years, I've done everything you've asked me to do and you never gave me a goat to celebrate with my friends all of this time." His father looked at him with compassion, extended his hands, and said, "My son, my dear son, you have always been with me and faithfully by my side and I am very thankful for that. You see, your brother was once lost and now he is found. Your brother, was once dead and now he is alive. Please, come inside. It is right and fitting that we celebrate today.

> *"The difference between fiction and reality is that fiction has to make sense."*
>
> —Tom Clancy

If you would like to read the original version of the story, it can be found in any Christian Bible in Luke 15:11-32 .

The spiritual context of this parable is to demonstrate a father's (image of God) unconditional love and compassion (open hand) he has for his children (humanity).

Get off Your High Horse and Walk.

This story is very powerful for me personally because I have so often played both roles of the brothers and I am now just learning how to play the role of the father.

I selected this story for the book because it beautifully reflects the journey of the ego. This parable can happen within you. Your ego Stage Manager plays the role of the lost son, the brother is your ego's "Personal Judge," and your true essence plays the role of the waiting father.

> *We would rather be ruined than changed.*
> *We would rather die in our dread*
> *Than climb the cross of the present*
> *And let our illusions die*
> —W.H.Auden

Did you notice the compassion the father had to the returning son? It is with the same love and the same compassion, your arms outstretched, that you can embrace your ego. There is no force or fighting. Abraham Lincoln said, "A house divided cannot stand." The same is true when we choose not to divide ourselves anymore.

Note that the son needed time to come to his senses. The father did not reject his son nor did he go after him and force him to return. He waited. Time is your friend and will stand by your side. Your work is to extend the invitation (open hand) with all of your love and compassion.

Are you starting to get the idea of how important open compassion is? Choosing not to judge or label others and yourself opens new possibilities in relationships, especially that between you and your ego.

It is important not to detach, yet not to give up on yourself and other people. When I think back on my life, there are many ugly times where I did not like myself for the way I was acting. I felt as if I was trapped in a place that I did not want to be. I would venture a guess that you too have had times or periods during your life where you also felt stuck. I would also imagine that there may have been someone who did not give up on you, believed enough in you to stand by your side. Try to remember "how" that person connected with you and how that person reached you. What did they do or say that broke through to you? I propose that that person was most certainly authentic in that they succeeded in reaching you, and they used love to do so.

Leveling the playing field

Here is an easy and effective way to balance your energy when dealing with people. If I feel close to empty, energy-wise,

> *Peace comes from within. Do not seek it without.*
> —Buddha

I find myself wanting to pull in and conserve the energy I have. It is tempting for me to project an image or to avoid people altogether.

I'd always wondered why I feel uncomfortable around certain people. My first observation was that the less we had in common, the more uncomfortable I felt. My second observation was what happened when dealing with people of higher status and authority.

The answer presented itself in the slums of Nairobi, Kenya. I was on a personal quest with only the objective to get to know the people of Kenya. I listened to the stories of people, and many of the stories led me to the slums. That was where I felt comfortable. The throngs of children holding my legs and my arms brought out the best in me. (I noticed that with children, there was absolutely no "trying" to be who I was.)

I met with the Japanese ambassador and the former ambassador of Kenya to Japan, who was the president of Toyota for East Africa. They were interested in hearing the impact that Kenya and the people had on me. My ego was at work, prompting me to project an image for them.

"Why would they be interested in hearing experiences from a person like me?" Sound familiar? I imagined that the ambassador was my own child, and it did not matter that he was Japanese and older than me. I looked into his eyes and imagined him as a child and then took the second step and imagined him as my child.

This immediately shifted my energy. I felt much more comfortable with him, and I noticed that he was smiling and at ease. Soon, we were both laughing. I took this experience into other parts of my life. I tried it on people that I did not know on the metro system. I tried it on homeless people in Barcelona. It always seemed to work.

> *We need to find the courage to say NO to the things and people that are not serving us if we want to rediscover ourselves and live our lives with authenticity.*
>
> —Barbara de Angelis

This is an example of transforming energy into compassion, and it is very effective. Try it.

Cutting yourself free - The best Sneech on the beach

Imagine you are on a boat that cannot move, because the anchor is stuck in the deep, dark waters below. No matter what you try, you can't manage to break free. Now imagine that you see a knife gleaming on deck, and you bend down and pick it up. You cut the cord that holds your boat captive.

Cut yourself free from as many unnecessary organizations and groups as you can. This is similar to going through your spare room or garage and cleaning it out. All organizations formed with a fundamental idea and gained power from the individuals buying into it. Every organization that you belong to requires the energy of its members to sustain it, which includes you. It is your responsibility to choose carefully the organizations that you can authentically belong to with good conscience.

If you haven't read *The Sneeches* by Dr. Seuss, please do. The story focuses on two types of Sneeches, one group who had bellies with stars and another who had no stars. The ones who did not have a star so wanted to belong to the group that did. One day, a smart critter named Sylvester McMonkey McBean offered to fix their problem by putting stars on their bellies for a small price. This critter exploited the Sneeches' need to belong and made a business out of it. In the end, no one could tell the differences between the Sneeches, because some had three, two, one, or no stars on their bellies. There was no better group to belong to because they were all mixed up and the Sneeches were left without a cent. Sylvester McMonkey McBean was crafty enough to see the Sneeches' insecurities and, like so many people today, profit from their fears.

> *Do what you can, with what you have, where you are*
> —Theodore Roosevelt

The Sneeches illustrate how people want to belong to something based on association. They think, "If I belong to this group, I must be OK." Consider to what groups and organizations you belong, and ask yourself why you belong to them.

There are other ways to cut yourself free. When you make a major purchase, observe your motivations for wanting what you want. How much of your decision is being driven by your image? You know who is driving your image, don't you? If being "successful" and having prestige and/or power are important to you, do not stop there. Ask yourself, what is my motivation to be "successful"?

Remember that organizations can be a collective projection of a false image. By joining organizations where your motivation is to gain approval and acceptance, you put up roadblocks that will make it difficult to travel down the road of authenticity.

Let go

Let go of the need to have all the answers and your need for control.

Do you remember how easy you were to impress when you were a child? Do you remember the way you felt when "going with the flow"? Say to yourself, "I am open to learning again. I don't have all the answers, I release control. I am open to surprise and to awe and to things much bigger than I am." (God-Universe)

Gift giving

There is a good feeling that comes from giving to others, isn't there? The best gift is to authentically receive.

Let us move to a higher perspective where we can observe an exchange in progress. As you watch the exchange in the following story, notice who is giving and who is receiving. Here is the question: Which is more difficult, to give or to receive? Who has the power?

> *The truth is that our finest moments are most likely to occur when we are feeling deeply uncomfortable, unhappy, or unfulfilled. For it is only in such moments, propelled by our discomfort, that we are likely to step out of our ruts and start searching for different ways or truer answers.*
>
> —Morgan Scott Peck

This reminds me of a story of a woman who lived in a small Midwestern town. She was always in control and never seemed to need the assistance of anyone. She was a pleasant, polite, and active woman who lived in her community, and was always giving to everyone. You would think that she would be well integrated into her community. But she felt very isolated and not accepted.

One Sunday, she was walking from her home to the open-air market where the entire community bought and sold fresh produce. She was almost there when she fell, twisting her ankle, falling on a jagged rock and dislocated her knee. Everyone in the market heard her cry, saw her on the street clutching her leg, and ran to give her assistance. "Leave me alone!" she screamed.

Although she was powerless and in extreme pain, everyone backed off a step. She saw on their faces the pain of being rejected in her time of need. A mixture of sadness and awareness overtook her. She said, "I'm sorry, I don't know how to accept help" and began to cry. The people she had rejected moments before were allowed in.

She said that on that day, she started to let down her "wall." She understood that receiving requires much more power than giving.

> *Each of us is something of a schizophrenic personality, tragically divided against ourselves.*
> —Martin Luther King, Jr.

Who has the true power? The one who gives or the one who receives? This woman gave a big gift by letting others assist her. This acceptance completes the energy cycle and allows balance, like a breath moving in and out. Only when you can truly receive will your giving be balanced and authentic.

How authentic are you with gift giving? What do you expect back? Examine your motivations for giving. Practice giving small gifts with no strings attached. Try to allow the authentic gifts that come your way. It can be as small as an authentic smile or as big as an authentic acknowledgment. Take a moment before you reply, allow yourself to feel the feeling, and respond only with what comes naturally and authentically.

Learn to want what you already have

Funerals have a way of catapulting many people directly to their life gift. I find that funerals are one of the few places where people are most authentic. Apart from the grieving that accompanies loss, there is something very alive to be felt.

> *If you don't change your beliefs, your life will be like this forever. Is that good news?*
>
> —Dr. Robert Anthon

When sitting in a funeral or wake service, I listen to wonderful stories and beautiful things said about the character of the person that passed on. The saddest part of the funeral is thinking about how much the person who died would have benefited from experiencing the love and affirmations while he or she was alive. I cannot miss the impact the loss of this person has on the people sitting around me. I often wonder if the person knew how much she or he meant to so many.

What stops me from being authentic with the people I love? If I knew my death was near, I would witness years of personal strife, conflict, and guilt melt away in seconds.

This thought has moved me to take action that makes a difference in my life with the people that are now living. It has a way of cutting through the thick walls that separate us.

This exercise has two parts. This first part has to do with shifting lower-level energies and emotions such as, guilt, blame, anger, and apathy into higher-level energies and emotions such as, empathy, love, and compassion. There is a temptation to get stuck and not see out of current situations where you have conflict. Your perspective is significantly narrowed, and options are few.

Start by bringing to mind the people you are most in conflict with, and see where you get stuck progressing toward resolution. How do you feel when you bring this person to mind? Are you constricted? Do you want to punish the person in some way? Do you want the person to feel your pain? Try to feel all the feelings that this person evokes in you.

Now imagine that you have one week to live. What is so important now? What is different all of a sudden? Has something shifted? What happened to all the power this person was holding over you a second before? The sobering reality of your mortality drop-kicks you directly and efficiently to your life gift.

Attention: Your life cycle has already been activated

This may be motivation for you. The average human lives approximately 25,000 days, which means that your "life bathtub" will be filled approximately that many times. You're author has already cycled his bathtub 15,705 times. Jiminy Christmas, I'm already halfway done! The big point here is that I may be done tomorrow. What we need to concern ourselves with is how we choose to direct our vital life-giving energy.

> Some writers confuse authenticity, which they ought always to aim at, with originality, which they should never bother about.
>
> —W. H. Auden quotes

I had the honor to walk with people on their way to their death.

When I was nineteen years old, I fell into a deep hole of depression that lasted for three years. I withdrew from everyone and had to search for a reason to live. It was during that time that I learned the darkest part of humanity. A priest saw me struggling and started walking with me through this "dark time." His name was Father Rick Arkfeld, and he was being eaten alive by cancer. He had every type of cancer you could imagine: lung, liver, blood, bone. He invited me—a skinny kid who looked like hell—to

Get off Your High Horse and Walk.

accompany him as he gave a series of talks about death and dying.

He was happier that anyone I have ever known, and he laughed all the time. He brought me out to his grave site, where his tombstone was already set and engraved; it said, "See, I told you I was sick"! He explained that positive humor has great power, and he wanted to give this gift to anyone who visited his grave. He asked me, as a joke, after he died, to run a bright orange extension cord from his grave to some nearby bushes. He wanted to have fun with people and make them wonder what he had down there when they passed by. I couldn't understand how a person whose days were counted could be so happy and able to joke about it. He said, "Slade, I want to say something to you, and I wanted to wait until we were standing here before I did so. Look at me, days before my death, and I am happy and full of life. Look at you. You have your full life ahead of you, and you are acting like you are already dead."

> *So much of the stress you hold and the ways you keep yourself stuck have to do with how far you've traveled from your original self. You can release that tension by identifying who's actually there under all those layers and why that pure essence is really perfect as it is...*
> —Jean Haner

He took me out to dinner that night, and said, "Slade, I want you to live your life not knowing that you have another day to live. Let me tell you a story, and maybe you will be able to understand.

"There was a small Indian boy who was coming of age. The chief and the elders of the tribe blindfolded him and led him on a long walk, shifting and changing direction often. The boy knew they had led him deep into a forest by the sounds of the animals. They finally came to a halt, and the chief spoke. 'You are a boy tonight who will die. Tomorrow we will return here to find the man in your place. You will leave your blindfold on until you can no longer hear us. We give you no weapon except for what has been given to you at birth.' Without another word, the chiefs and elders walked off in different directions.

"The boy was petrified. The forest was so dark that it made no difference that he removed his blindfold. He heard animals of every sort around him. He grabbed a stone, clutched it to his chest, and curled up against a shrub, hoping to escape the notice of wolves or Indians from other tribes. He dozed off, and when he woke he saw the beginning outlines of the trees against the sky. He sighed a big breath of relief, and then he stopped! His breath caught in his throat, as he noticed not three paces away from him a huge Indian, standing there silently. He could see enough to know this Indian was a warrior, and if he noticed him, his death would be certain and swift.

> ... *when you let go of that stress when you can stop blaming yourself for being who you are, it frees up an enormous amount of energy to move forward in life.*
>
> —Jean Haner

"Not moving a muscle, breathing as shallow as a tortoise, he lay there hoping to escape notice. The sky continued to brighten, giving details to the forest and the warrior who was poised in front of him, still waiting. The boy was readying himself to accept death or to try to fight, when he finally rose and looked at the warrior. No! It couldn't be! He saw that the warrior was his father. He screamed, 'Daddy!' and ran to him, burying his head in his chest, and he began to cry wildly. Through his sobs the boy asked how and why. The father held him and replied, 'Don't you know that you are my boy and that I would never let anything harm to you as long as I am living? You are a man now, and you will always be my little boy.'"

Get off Your High Horse and Walk.

I had tears in my eyes as Father Rick said, "Here is your answer to your question. What kind of spirituality do you have? Is your God a tyrant wanting to cause harm, blame, to hurt, to punish and hurt people? I give this gift to you, Slade. It's time for you to open your eyes to see who stands next to you." He told me of the God that he loved. After he was finished, he also had tears in his eyes. "This is why I smile and laugh in the face of death. I embrace every moment of life that I have, and right now I have a friend in front of me who really wants to live and laugh."

> *There is nothing wrong with you. Be Who You Are.*
> —Robin Rice

Father Rick did not die right away. His cancer went into total remission and, through his talks; he continued to prepare people to live. He died a few years later due to a heart attack.

I climbed out of the depression with a new perspective of spirituality that felt right. I truly understand that experience is the best instructor. I understand things now that I would not have been able to without experiencing them. If someone were to appear with a magic wand and say, "I can transport you back in time before the depression took place, and I can spare you the deep sorrow and despair that you experienced all those years," I would say, "No thank you." I now understand that some of my skills and abilities to see deeply and feel for others around me have come from suffering.

Who is Slade Suiter? He's an instructor, therapist, a philosopher, and a speaker. Oh really?

That is what he does. I will ask you again: Who is he? He's a composite of his experiences and the choices he made while he was alive. Does that include his failures? Yes, and it turns out that his failures turned out to be his greatest successes by his choice to be himself no matter the cost. Wow! How cool.

We are all living experiences with a unique thumbprint. We all live under the same sky and breathe the same air. We all have been given the same gift of this bathtub that we draw from daily.

> *The authentic self is the soul made visible.*
> —Sarah Ban Breathnach

Do not shortchange yourself, trying to push away unpleasant experiences that you have had or others around you. Allow yourself to be human. Accept all the feelings that come along with your experiences. Accept all the teachings and insights. When you do not have to pretend, you can clearly see things as they happen. Own the good, the bad, and the ugly. They are all available for you to grow from.

Cleaning out the wolves and vampires

You have seen the enormous amount of energy that you can save by not projecting a false image. You also are aware that like energy provokes like energy. I have noticed in my life that there were many "wolves in sheep clothing" and "vampires" who were claiming to be my friends or acquaintances wanting to stay actively in my life.

"Wolves" are people who hide behind the image that they project. These people are competitive and aggressive. They need to always have the last word, to always be right, and when the time is right, they will turn and bite you in the back.

"Vampires" are people who suck vital energy from those around them, and the "blood" is your esteem and approval. They seek their identity outside of themselves. They will do anything in order to suck on the blood of your esteem to validate themselves.

Wolves are easy to spot, because they are territorial and opportunistic in their feeding (needing energy from others). If you find yourself constantly dancing around someone out of fear of possibly upsetting them, chances are you have a wolf in your presence. The wolves look for opportunities to build themselves up on the demise of others (Cat's Claw). Wolves characteristically prefer to attack from the back, they gossip like no other. Be warned, you are also fair prey when your back is turned.

> *Live dangerously; take risks; cultivate eccentricity, which means growing closer to being yourself. This will give you a life worth living and of which you can be proud.*
>
> —Thomas D. Willhite

Vampires are more difficult to spot; they are more likely to be felt. Mental and emotional exhaustion are characteristic symptoms as a result of a vampire feeding on your vital life energy. Individuals who embody characteristics of vampires are most likely to exhibit Cry Me a River (The Professional Victim).

I want to make a note here: I find it important to clarify that cleaning out wolves and vampires from your lives does not mean that you stop respecting and loving these individuals. It is a simple recognition of the love and respect that you have for yourself coupled with an active decision of who you "choose" to travel your life with.

This can and should be done without judgment or need to punish them. Ask yourself, how does this relationship serve my path toward authenticity? How many times will I need to be bitten and drained before realizing that this relationship is unhealthy for both of us?

If the wolf or vampire is in your personal circle (work, family or friends), use common sense. Talk first, share your truth with the wolf or vampire and the impact they are having on you. Try "declawing the cat" in this next section. If that does not work then you can begin to distance yourself in a healthy way.

Choosing to travel with positive and well-intentioned people in your life, while not judging and respecting everyone are vital ingredients that will help you on your road to authenticity.

Declawing the cat

You can say what you mean and mean what you say without being mean. Be direct, and hold people accountable for the impact of their words.

Here is a tip that may help you in the next Cat's Claw attack. When someone intentionally attacks you, you can say, "What was your intention behind that comment?" or "I assume that you have a second intention behind what you said. Is this true?" or "Your statement had two meanings: what you said, and what you did not say, which can be inferred. Did you mean this?"

> *"Only the truth of who you are, if realized, will set you free."*
> —Eckhart Tolle

You are drawing new boundaries. You are saying, "I am not going to accept these attacks anymore." The first confrontation can be uncomfortable, but it bolsters your self-respect. Practice with a friend. Find your calm, assertive, nonjudgmental voice.

There is no need to mount your high horse again.

You are OK as you are, and you are something! Who needs a horse when you can walk in the shoes of your authenticity?

Environment

Situations and environments can suck out vital energy and retard creativity. How creative are you when you are sitting in a disorganized mess, or an environment charged with passive-aggressive poison?

Does your environment help or distract you from staying present and authentic? Sometimes you do not have complete control over your environment, but when you do, choose places that enhance your life. Be creative, clean your house, go to the library, and go into nature when you can. These work for me. What works for you?

Living someone else's legacy

Whenever we set out to fulfill the expectations of someone else without consciously making it our own, it is a lie. It can be as minor as picking up a room or as serious as marrying someone your parents approve of or going to college and studying something that is not your passion. You live your life according to external expectations. The actions may not be bad in themselves; the problem is when we do them for approval or out of fear. Who owns your dream, and whose energy are you using to get there? It is important to consciously decide on a course of action from your truth. When your identity and beliefs are aligned, you "fill your own shoes," and where you walk is entirely your decision.

> *Accepting the reality of our sinfulness means accepting our authentic self. Judas could not face his shadow; Peter could. The latter befriended the impostor within; the former raged against him.*
> —Brennan Manning

Do not be afraid to bring your beliefs to your test of authenticity. Why do I believe this? Do I really believe this? Is it me, or was I taught this when I was young? Open every drawer in your "skeleton closet." If you hear yourself say, "I don't know if I do," that is fine. Remember that time is your friend, and your truth is growing just like you. Open yourself to learning more, listening to others, and trusting your intuition.

This is how your spiritual self becomes healthy. Can you imagine how many wars could be avoided if everyone could do this?

Let's talk about sex

Sex is a subject where a lot of us feel stuck. Many of us project an image of what we should be or how we should feel as sexual beings. Sex is a potent part of being a human, and it would be silly for us to overlook such a wonderful part of ourselves.

Let's follow sex through the model and review the following types: Ditto Bug, Head in the Sand, Prostitutes Are Us, The Small God, and Drama Queen/King. By looking at the models side by side, we can get the sense that when we are on the left side of the model, sex feels unbalanced, unnatural, and forced. I may feel as if I am trying to force myself to be something different than I really am. Ditto Bug frequently shows up ("I am acting how I was taught to act.") Society and cultural pressures weigh heavily on how we think we are "supposed" to be.

> *Think wrongly, if you please, but in all cases think for yourself.*
>
> —Doris Lessing

It seems logical for the ego to want to wrap so much identity and energy into sex. Society invests a large amount of time, money, and resources in setting up sexual norms and expectations for us to fulfill. The bottom line, on the left side of the model, is that we are not good enough as we are. We must always strive to project an image, to ourselves and others, that we are normal and fulfilling society's expectations. Our validation is external.

The left side of the model is a haven for self-blame and guilt. Your ego can justify abuse of power (mental, emotional and physical), which comes from a failure to recognize and respect others' boundaries. You feel the need to control yourself or others. Be aware that the unbalanced side offers a place to hide, and many people find excuses to "not show up" or to shut down a vital part of ourselves.

Sex seems to make sense only in the right side of the model, where we feel a sense of balance, integration, communication, and connection. Sex seems to be transformed and accepted for what it is. There is no need to try or compare (size, frequency, kinky, amount, with whom, etc.). It is simply enough just to be. A sense of humor goes a long way to deflate posturing and egos. Your personal ethics are integrated into the right side of the model, and this is where you have responsibility and sensitivity for your actions. This is where true communication can take place. This is a place where there is no room for guilt or judgment. The right side of the model contains integrity and the feeling that "I am OK just as I am."

> *To be nobody but myself-in a world which is doing its best, night and day, to make me somebody else-means to fight the hardest battle any human can fight, and never stop fighting.*
> —e.e. cummings

Get off the fence and get moving

Use your imagination in a vivid and active way. Do this using your ancient and essential language, then choose the best result and move forward into action.

Become aware of your body—any contraction, constriction, tightness in the stomach, slow or shallow breathing, a bad taste in the mouth. Then become aware of your body for expansion, warmth, soft tummy, a more profound and relaxed breathing. Try on these two scenarios—simulate trying on shoes before you purchase them. After that, decide which one fits you better.

Find a problem issue that you're working with. This exercise works well with a conflict or a big decision that you have been avoiding.

Give yourself full permission to use your imagination. See everything in vivid and exquisite detail. Your imagination provides a safe area to explore possibilities. You have permission to see and feel things and explore them without fear. The idea is to create an "almost awake dream" where you are conscious and able to make decisions.

Set a timer for five minutes.

Now think of a choice that you have in your life. It can be anything. Allow yourself to go "scientific." Act as if you were sincerely interested in only the best decision based on your authenticity. Choose to not judge yourself, and give yourself the freedom to explore all possibilities fully.

Do you see them? Now select one. Imagine that you have selected this choice in reality.

Ready? GO! Set the timer for five minutes again.

See and feel everything. You have chosen to go on this road. See yourself saying the words that you have chosen. See the reactions of the people around you; see yourself packing your bags, walking into the office, walking out of the office. How do you feel inside? Lighter? Constricted? Peaceful? Sad? Feel everything that is available to you, and do not mask anything.

> *What if the question is not why I am so infrequently the person I really want to be, but why do I so infrequently want to be the person I really am?*
>
> —Oriah Mountain Dreamer

Now select another option and repeat.

Now is the time to start trusting yourself again. Choose the path that felt the most right, the truest. Staying stuck is not an option anymore, because you know too much about your own truth. What if you make a mistake and choose the wrong path? So what! At least you're moving, and if it is the wrong path, you can learn from it.

Why have you not moved on this decision before? Was it fear? Would you have to say good-bye to something? Could it be that you were afraid of accountability? Were you uncomfortable? Could it be a way to avoid becoming successful?

If you have just experienced what feels right and best to you inside, and your authentic self resonates with that decision, what will stop you now? You have a choice to make: go or stay.

Make the decision to do it. You will be accountable for it, and this may take you way outside your comfort zone. You have spent way too much time there anyway!

It is time to be brave and make your own decisions.

Make this a life practice. Discipline yourself by using your imagination. Imagine, imagine, and imagine everything in your life. See yourself solving impossible situations. Imagine yourself in new situations. Change your occupation. Try on different approaches for resolving conflict with your spouse. How does it feel? If something feels wrong, trust it and try again. See your imagination as the primary tool to use from now on.

> *Authenticity is full acceptance of who you are.*
> —Inma Peñaranda

The more you practice this, the easier it will be to separate motivations from ego. It feels different than your truth. Be consistent and move.

Chapter Summary
- Get unstuck! The worst thing you can do is to remain stagnant. It is better to take a chance and move in the wrong direction than to remain stagnant—at least you will learn something.
- Break down walls or allow them to fall. Your sense of humor will give you the needed flexibility to counterbalance rigidity and resistance . It is impossible to laugh at yourself in a lighthearted way while maintaining rigidity.
- Learn from your failures. Do not be afraid to fall and fail. Failure is a great instructor and is essential to learning and growth.
- It's not all your ego's fault. Do not declare war on your ego. Refrain from using guilt, judgment, and shame. Lighten up, extend your hands in an open

invitation for your ego to come home and reintegrate with you.
- Level the playing field. A wonderful way to disable the inferior and superior self lies is seeing yourself in the eyes of others. Look into the eyes of another person and imagine him or her as your son or daughter, sister or brother, and see what happens with your energy around that person. This neutralizes the fear of difference.
- Cut yourself free. Let go! What and who you associate with can put hooks in you that prevent you from moving forward on your road to authenticity. Cut yourself free from the unnecessary organizations in your life.

> *"Honesty and transparency make you vulnerable. Be honest and transparent anyway."*

- The greatest gift that you can give others is to learn how to truly receive.
- Learn to want what you already have. Relearn to appreciate your life. Notice what becomes important when you become aware of the life that you have right now.
- All you need to concern yourself with is how you choose to direct your vital life-giving energy.
- Clean out the werewolves and vampires so that friends are true friends. Have love and compassion for all, and choose wisely who you travel with. Find the true friends who will support you on your road to authenticity.
- Declaw the cats in your life. Respect flows both directions. It is easy to respect others; however, it is equally important to respect yourself and to establish boundaries in a way that is nonjudgmental, assertive, and calm.

- Live your own legacy, not someone else's. Go through all of your beliefs, one by one, to look at everything that you believe in. Separate what you were told to believe from what you authentically believe.
- Sex is part of the ancient language. What version of sex do you prefer? Sex on the unbalanced side of the model, or sex on the balance side of the model? What feels right for you?
- Get off the fence and get moving. Make choices and decisions that direct your life. Actively address conflicts and decisions that you have been avoiding by using your imagination.

"No legacy is so rich as honesty."
—Shakespeare

Conclusion

Don't fool yourself—you know too much now to go back into your life of fantasy and lies. You are not a small god; you are alive and mortal. You do not have your head in the sand. You are aware and conscious of your ego. How refreshing it is to rediscover your authentic self, to see yourself as you really are. How freeing it is to know that you do not have to try to be yourself. It is natural and automatic. The only work you need to do is to choose to dissociate yourself from your deep-seated self-deception.

> *"If you tell the truth you don't have to remember anything."*
> —Mark Twain

Listen to the power of this paragraph:

"I am alive right now. I am something. I am OK just as I am, including my weaknesses, flaws, and failures. I am not alone. I am connected to God-Universe and everyone and everything alive. I am present and receptive and have nothing to prove to others. I choose not to judge or label. I feel and experience my truth and hear my intuition. I want to create from this expansive place, and my passion stirs me to action. Happiness is a mere byproduct of pursuing my truth. I am not the slave of my emotions. Life's extremes and polarities are available for me to draw upon at my will; the dance of balance has meaning here. I am fully animal, alive, impulsive, and instinctual. I am pure spirit, called with an urge and desire to create. I am part of you and all life. My truth is growing just as I am. I do not mind standing out as long as it is my authentic self who is the one standing. I laugh, I am human, and at home."

Wow! Did you like it? I loved it!!

Get off Your High Horse and Walk.

If you find yourself jumping on a stage to perform out of habit, relax, it is no big deal. Climb off the stage, wag your finger at your ego, and say, "Ahh ahh ahh, not this time." Know that guilt, shame, anger turned toward yourself are your ego's favorite tools. You will go a long way on your path to authenticity by using your sense of humor; it neutralizes the poison that guilt, shame, and anger once fed you.

> *"To find yourself, think for yourself."*
> —Socrates

When you have a victory over your ego, celebrate. Take note every time you choose your truth over a lie. Celebrate no matter how small the victory, and feel what it feels like to reclaim small pieces of yourself.

You are a lock and a key, and when you return to your essential self, you become unlocked. All the learning that you have accumulated through your life experience becomes a key for yourself as well as others who will benefit from hearing your truth. You will help others to unlock their truth just as other people have keys that will help you.

You no longer need to seek approval or validation. You are free, and no one has power over you except for those you give power to. If your vital life energy is not spent in projecting and defending a false image, you have plenty of energy and can choose how to use it.

Be as kind to yourself as you are to others. Grant yourself the same hospitality and forgiveness that you would give to others. If there is drama in your life, let it be there by choice, not by default.

Your spirituality and your connection to God-Universe becomes like breathing. You rediscover how to authentically receive and how to authentically give, and because you can now see yourself in others, labeling and prejudice don't make sense. The ingredients for love are there.

Conclusion

You are one among millions, and the coolest part is that each one of those millions needs you. They need you because you are holding that exclusive key that is only accessible when you allow yourself to be authentically you. The energy of this interaction between you and the world is receptive in nature. There is no need to defend only one outcome, allowing you to be open to various possibilities. The authentic self naturally generates a higher emotional frequency that the world returns to you based on the law of attraction.

You now know that everything is a choice and you are responsible for the direction you choose. You no longer have the luxury of the ignorance that is required for victims to exist in. Your experience is now your guide and if you choose to maintain your world of lies or return to your authenticity, you are free to choose. You have the awesome responsibility and freedom of choosing the direction of your life.

> *"There is no wisdom save in truth."*
> —Martin Luther

Stay congruent with your thoughts, feelings, and emotions. Work with calm and assertive energy. If you fail, do not be harsh. Rise again, and relax back into your true self. You have nothing to prove to others , no need to gain their approval. You know too much now for you to climb back on your high horse.

Request

It may be unorthodox to include a request page, but because this book is about authenticity, I felt that this was a fun and necessary way to express myself.

If you enjoyed this book and found it helpful, please make sure it finds its way to someone who needs it.

If you have friends who are good publishers, send this book to them. I want to expand access to this book as much as possible.

> "What is true is invisible to the eye. It is only with the heart that one can see clearly."
> —Antoine de Saint-Exupery

Many of the ideas that I tie together have come from great authors, philosophers, and people who have been working on the concept of "awareness and presence." Eckhart Tolle wrote about the importance of "presence" and living in the now. Miguel Ruiz wrote books about the agreements that we make in our life that either tie us up or free us. He also wrote about dissociating ourselves from our lies. Marianne Williamson offers a clear interpretation of *A Course in Miracles*. In *Power versus Force*, Dr. David Hawkins speaks about studies that have calibrated emotional frequencies and the impact we have on ourselves and others when we live in a particular emotional frequency.

If you happen to be friends with Marianne Williamson, Miguel Ruiz, Dr. Hawkins, Eckhart Tolle, and singer Alanis Morissette, please set up a coffee or dinner date for me.

I will make the trip. These authors and artists have inspired me deeply.

If you would like further information on the subject of authenticity, or future books in progress, I invite you to contact me at www.sladesuiter.com.

Bibliography

Arbinger Institute. *The Anatomy of Peace: Resolving the Heart of Conflict*. San Francisco: Berrett-Koehler Publishing Inc., 2006.

Hawkins, David R. *Power versus Force: The Hidden Determinants of Human Behavior*. Carlsbad, CA: Hay House, 2002.

Lao Tsu. *Tao Te Ching*. Translated by Gia-Fu Feng and Jane English. New York: Vintage Books, Inc., 1997.

Ruiz, Miguel Angel. *The Four Agreements: A Practical Guide to Personal Freedom*. San Rafael, CA: Amber-Allen Publishing, 2001.

Ruiz, Miguel Angel and Janet Mills. *The Voice of Knowledge*. San Rafael, CA: Amber-Alan Publishing Inc., 2004.

Tolle, Eckhart. *The Power of Now: A Guide to Spiritual Enlightenment*. Novato, CA: Namaste Publishing and New World Library, 2004.

Williamson, Marianne. *A Return to Love: Reflections on the Principals of a Course in Miracles*. New York: Harper Perennial Publishers, Inc., 1993.

Theodore Seuss. *The Sneeches and Other Stories*. New York: Random House, Inc., 1961.

Contacts:
Dr. Michelle Nielson: www.drmichellenielsen.com
Albert Lobo (Graphic Illustrator) albertlobo1981@yahoo.es
Carien Everwijn (Horse Whisperer) carien.everwijn@wanadoo.nl
Slade Suiter (Myself) Slade@sladesuiter.com

Biography

Slade Suiter was born in Omaha, Nebraska, in 1966.

He received a liberal arts education from the University of Nebraska at Omaha and University of Nebraska at Lincoln, graduating from the University of St. Thomas in St. Paul, Minnesota, with a degree in speech communication with a minor in philosophy.

He attended St. John Vianney Seminary and School of Divinity in St. Paul, Minnesota.

He is a CTI Coaching Training Institute-trained leader and coactive life coach. He has traveled to Asia, Africa, Europe, and the Middle East, giving workshops and seminars. He has a passion for sitting down to listen to people's stories.

His inspiration is working on rediscovery and teaching others to rebuild on the foundation of authenticity.

www.ingramcontent.com/pod-product-compliance
Lightning Source LLC
Chambersburg PA
CBHW061445040426
42450CB00007B/1227